Levinas and Theology

Philosophy and Theology series

Other titles in the Philosophy and Theology series include:

Adorno and Theology, Christopher Craig Brittain
Badiou and Theology, Frederiek Depoortere
Derrida and Theology, Steven Shakespeare
Foucault and Theology, Jonathan Tran
Girard and Theology, Michael Kirwan
Habermas and Theology, Maureen Junker-Kenny
Hegel and Theology, Martin J. De Nys
Kant and Theology, Pamela Sue Anderson and Jordan Bell
Kierkegaard and Theology, Murray Rae
Nietzsche and Theology, Craig Hovey
Vattimo and Theology, Thomas G. Guarino
Wittgenstein and Theology, Tim Labron
Žižek and Theology, Adam Kotsko

Levinas and Theology

Nigel Zimmermann

B L O O M S B U R Y
LONDON • NEW DELHI • NEW YORK • SYDNEY

Bloomsbury T&T Clark

An imprint of Bloomsbury Publishing Plc

50 Bedford Square   175 Fifth Avenue
London   New York
WC1B 3DP   NY 10010
UK   USA

www.bloomsbury.com

First published 2013

© Nigel Zimmermann, 2013

British Library Cataloguing-in-Publication Data
A catalogue record for this book is available from the British Library.

ISBN: HB: 978-0-567-60652-5
PB: 978-0-567-24867-1

Library of Congress Cataloging-in-Publication Data
Zimmermann, Nigel
Levinas and Theology/Nigel Zimmermann p.cm
Includes bibliographic references and index.
ISBN 978-0-567-60652-5 (hardcover) – ISBN 978-0-567-24867-1 (pbk.)
2012045678

Typeset by Deanta Global Publishing Services, Chennai, India
Printed and bound in India

Contents

Preface   vi

1 Introduction: The Provocation of Levinas   1

2 Being's Other   13

3 '*Would* You Like to Do a Bit of Theology?'
   Levinas and the *Theological Turn*   41

4 The Disturbance of Theology   69

5 Preferring the Shadows:
   The 'Little Faith' of Israel   97

6 The Return of God?   127

7 Conclusion   157

Notes   167
Bibliography   187
Index   195
Biblical References   199

Preface

It is a privilege to contribute to this book series, in which various philosophers are introduced to theologians. It is more than an introduction, but it cannot be said to form a comprehensive review. Only key ideas can be highlighted in such a book, but they have nonetheless been thought through with sensitivity to Levinas' thought, which is deemed only fitting. Levinas does not offer the kind of systematic writing that lends itself to unambiguous clarity and order. He writes to issue an appeal to his readers on philosophical grounds. His is the conspicuously French approach that undertakes a provocation in the mind of the reader. I have sought to explain the nature of this provocation as it pertains to the theological task, and no doubt there will be theologians who take offence, or deem Levinas an unwelcome dialogue partner. This raises the question of the nature and mission of theology, and such a point of conjecture is an argument worth having. Indeed, I do not propose that Levinas be a partner to theology analogous to marriage, or some equally thoroughgoing commitment. Rather, Levinas may be a partner for the purposes of something like a dance; the foxtrot for example. This better conjures the nature of a partnership that might be thrilling, challenging, colourful and robust. It is more than flirtation, and less than a formal commitment, but with all the excitement of an act that is fast, rigorous and performed in the full public glare of the ballroom lights.

For the theologian, there are of course perplexing challenges in the work of Levinas, and there are also fruitful opportunities.

Specifically, this book defends the fruitfulness of theologians taking from Levinas the provocative turn towards alterity within the context of inter-subjectivity. The turn towards alterity is, as Levinas insists, an ethical moment. Otherness is not laid bare like the flat surface of a holiday postcard, but is a dynamic experience of difference in human affairs. It has a universal significance and theology is not to be quietly excused from such a discovery. As I argue, such a turn challenges theology to regain the en-wondered sense of ethical import in the face of the other, and to 'sober up' in the bright sunlight of truth's appearing. In this sense, it is a very public and indeed social fruit that is cultivated.

Theologians are, therefore, challenged to consider carefully their vocation. The self-identification of the God of the Hebrew Scriptures in the person of Christ ought to provoke in the theologian cautious self-inspection. In Christ, the same alterity that raised the prophets and took claim upon the people of Israel is given in the warm flesh of frail humanity. It is a paradoxical realization of alterity in that its claim is both a strong one, even as it sits radically open to the violence of the world. In the New Testament, examples of God's glory (the Transfiguration, the miracles, the Resurrection) contrast with Christ's passion and crucifixion, and the tragic humanity of a narrative that includes loss, heartbreak, death and loneliness. The cross of Golgotha must have its place in the terrain of Christian theology, or else it cannot be a Christian theology at all. This is a conviction the Reformers perceived correctly; that a *theologia crucis* does not destroy the divine claims of Christ, but reveals his divinity in a significant way. In the New Testament, the divine claim of Christ is continually linked to the God of Abraham, Isaac and Jacob (see Acts 3:13). In other words, the law of the old reaches a new threshold in the personification of God's action in Christ: 'For the law was given through Moses; grace and truth came through Jesus Christ' (John 1:17).

I recognize that to link the claims above to the Levinasian purchase upon alterity in the face of the other person is to embark upon a certain risk. It risks both the integrity of Christian theology and the nuance of Levinas' work. Having recognized the risk, I do, however, maintain that the integrity of theology is only strengthened and fortified by a hospitable encounter with Levinas, and that the philosopher can be read carefully and rigorously, and often critically. This book cannot detail every nuance and variable notion that makes an appearance in Levinas' work. Moreover, it falls outside its remit for this book to attempt a full and probing account of Levinas' entire corpus, or its place in the history of philosophy. Other thinkers are progressing in these important tasks already. Rather, this book thinks through Levinas from a theological perspective, and gives an account of how theologians have already handled his challenging thought. It is written with a debt to those theologians who are already wrestling with him, and I sincerely apologize to those who have been overlooked or dealt with in a limited fashion. Time and space are authentic limitations. Given the target audience of an English-speaking readership, attention has been granted to Levinas commentators who are English-language writers or translated into English, and therefore widely available.

Much has been written already on the philosophy of Levinas. Less so on his theology, or perhaps more accurately, where theology finds itself *after* Levinas. A number of important texts will be looked at in this book which, in various ways, have attempted to rectify this aporia in contemporary theology. Chiefly however, I will pursue the following objectives:

1. Indicate the essential contours of Levinas' thought as they relate to the concerns of theology; especially in their permutations concerning God, revelation and religion.
2. Contextualize Levinas in the light of the difficult circumstances of the Holocaust and their demanding purchase upon him and others of that generation.
3. Recognize positively the Jewish springboard from which much of Levinas' philosophy and ethics are derived. This

is done fully cognizant of the author's own Christian faith, and the need to develop renewed ways of conceiving the relationship between Judaism and Christianity, and their various and diverse communities.

4. Articulate the provocation Levinas makes towards theology, and how it can be positively received, even if it means self-inspection and a new attentiveness to the vocational nature of the theologian. This I call the 'sobering up' of theology.

5. In relation to this previous objective, I take from Levinas the arrogating insistence that holy texts guide and animate one's life within the world. Scripture is opened up in Levinas, and its priorities remain as counter-cultural in the contemporary context as in the past.

6. Lastly, I have tried to open up Levinas to theologians as they reflect more deeply on how the above relate to their own task within religious and secular contexts. Indeed, the distinction between those contexts is rather muted by Levinas, in whom can be seen an approach to ethics that seems overbearing in its universality. Furthermore, the theologian discovers that theology has its own historical resources which are substantial in their own right, and made fruitful in an encounter with phenomenology.

The titles of the chapters speak for themselves, but in each I have maintained a commitment to the above objectives.

On a personal level, this book is written for God and my family. I am grateful to those whose involvement made it a tangible possibility. Thank you to Tom Kraft of Continuum for his initial invitation to produce this book, and the patience and detailed attention of both he and Anna Turton, and to all of the staff at Bloomsbury. My sincere thanks to the Wingate Foundation for seeing fit to fund this project and to the St Barnabas Society for their charity to a young theologian in need of assistance. A heartfelt thanks to Gladstone's Library in Hawarden and to the School of Divinity in the University of Edinburgh, each in its own way affording me generous space for writing in the beauty of Wales and Scotland, respectively.

Moreover, I thank my colleagues in the University of Notre Dame Australia for their encouragement as I finished this undertaking in the grittier surrounds of Sydney, which seems entirely fitting. My students also taught me much in these final writing stages about the character of the face-to-face. A heartfelt appreciation is offered to friends and colleagues who attentively shared their wisdom and critical thoughts: Jason Wardley, Joe Rivera, Michael Purcell, Michael Morgan, Matt Tan, Chris Hackett, Renée Köhler-Ryan and others. I am thankful to those scholars and theologians who spent time discussing and arguing about Levinas with me. I record an indebtedness to my parents who have the patience of Job. Of course, every written page is witness to a labour of time that may only be utilized when loved ones grant it willingly. Thank you to Christine, Dominic and Timothy.

Chapter 1

Introduction:
The Provocation of Levinas

La dimension du divin s'ouvre à partir du visage humain.
Emmanuel Levinas
Totalité et infini, Sect 1., B. 6

Emmanuel Levinas is one of the creative minds of the twentieth century. His contribution is counter-intuitive, and sits uneasily within established patterns of previous scholarship. The above words indicate Levinas' turn towards the other – the *Other* – in which, for him, the notion of divinity is witnessed in its trace. Levinas' thought is a provocation not simply to conceptual debate or reflection, but also to ethical responsibility. It has been some time now since he passed away, but his influence has in fact grown, and not only among scholars. This is true, even as a new century develops its own ethical challenges and moral outrages, and the human condition carries onwards in a disparaging lack of critical self-awareness or ethical reflection. With the expansion of Levinas' influence, it is important that theologians feel capable of addressing his thought with a degree of informed awareness. In what follows, this book offers a humble avenue for theologians to explore in gaining some framework in which to read and address the provocation made by Levinas.

It is helpful to note that during his own lifetime, Levinas did not make the 'splash' enacted by others around him, such as Jacques Derrida and Jean-Paul Sartre. Yet, as they both attest, Derrida's deconstructionism and Sartre's existentialism owe much to Levinas. Other thinkers owe similar debts to Levinas; John Paul II, Paul Ricœur, Jean-Luc Marion, Kevin Hart and others have drawn on Levinas' complex thought to aid in what, broadly, can be called the 'task of theology'. Having made such a general observation, it must be acknowledged that Levinas cannot easily be cushioned into the latter phenomenological and post-Husserlian categories that arose in the latter half of the twentieth century. He was not a deconstructionist. He was not an existentialist. Neither was he a nihilist. Yet he has tendencies in these categories that may better be understood in relation to his Jewish heritage, which remained both private and concrete throughout his life. He had a faith that did not lose sight of either its textual roots in the Torah or the Talmud, or the new vision his philosophy opened up onto God and the world. Levinas certainly saw himself as a phenomenologist, although even that is in dispute among some (see the debate about the 'theological turn' fostered by Dominique Janicaud and others).

Of centrality to reading Levinas is that his thought cannot be understood apart from his experience of World War II. In the Holocaust, he lost close family and friends, and his wife and daughter were only spared because of the intervention of Maurice Blanchot and the holy lies of nuns who hid Jews in a Catholic cloister; namely the Sisters of St Vincent de Paul in Prelfort. The terrible events of the Shoah affected every thinker who survived it, and no less so than the person of Levinas. Yet, his work is not in itself a philosophy of the Holocaust. Rather, it is a creative response to the horrors he witnessed, and an attempt to think otherwise than the kind of philosophy which, for Levinas, made the Holocaust possible. One text that was never finished, and which has only recently become available, is a novel Levinas began called *Triste Opulence* [Sad Opulence], later renamed *Eros*. Even in its incompleteness, it is a provocative read. In this unusual foray into fiction, Levinas is acutely aware of the complexity of erotic desire and the reduction of dignity that occurred in each of the persons who suffered or lost their lives at the hands of German National

Socialism. In an unnerving example, he depicts a train cabin carrying Jewish men towards a Nazi camp. Despite their entrapment and the sufferings they are already experiencing, their minds are presented as resisting a complete capitulation to the moment of present confinement. Out of the window they spy hanging a woman's undergarments, on display next to her home. As the train travels briskly onwards, the men witness a glimpse of this enticing scene, and they take to the window to leer and allow their imaginations to wander. This jars for the reader of the narrative. It seems somehow sickening that men in such circumstances could be distracted from their plight and seek something so unpromising as the faint imaginings of sexual gratification. Of course, the desire is fantastical, and the obstacles between the men and the woman are great; she is unknown and unheard, she may be married and off limits, it must be assumed that at least some of the men themselves are married and that none of them, under any circumstances, will even meet her.

Furthermore, the men are trapped not just by the walls and locks of the train cabin, but also by the incorporation of bureaucrats and soldiers into a broader systemic intrigue. The State itself had become the oppressor, and so the sudden erotic impulse, so closely aligned with sexual longing, is prevented from any possible fulfilment. The train carries on, even if imagination remains in the moment in which the men's eyes witness an object of enticement. Because the narrative of the Holocaust is so well known, a reader might be sickened to think of these men as they approach suffering and certain death, being distracted by an impossible dream. Nevertheless, Levinas' text spends a little time on the scene to illustrate a profound truth that is too easily overlooked; the excessive humanity of the men in question. These suffering men, while treated as subhuman, remain human to excess. Their humanity is surplus to the entrapment in which they find themselves, and is witnessed in the event of their imaginative longings. The men, in their embodied humanity, refuse the limits of their oppressors. Levinas, therefore, insists on his own refusal to implicate the men entirely into the anthropological categories of their oppressors, which of course see in them nothing but an animalistic, cancerous inhibitor of Germany and Europe's progress. Despite the Nazi persecution of these men, they remain fully human, which includes their sexual appetites and immature desires after that which will never be attained. Perhaps the non-attainability of the desire itself is a peculiarly human trait. The authentication of their humanity occurs in the sudden grip of sexual longing they experience, which exceeds the limitations of the present situation and therefore refuses the descriptions issued by their captors.

In *Eros*, Levinas explores his account of alterity, which is an otherness that cannot be circumvented – even by a train carriage journeying to genocide – and which means to convey the irreducibility of the *other* human person. The notion of humanity's excess is a repeated point of departure in Levinas' philosophical works, and it challenges the categories and formulations of Western philosophy in its traditional expressions. In this book on Levinas and theology, it is not argued that Levinas does anything so transient as to attempt a revolution in the way we think, but instead offers a phenomenological description of human inter-subjectivity that, in form and intention, stirs up an ethical response. Theologians, like any other readers, may well construct conceptual language to refuse the import of Levinas into their thought, but in no way can he be ignored with impunity. Furthermore, it will be argued that theologians may find in Levinas a provocation to work more rigorously within their own broad tradition, and to exploit the richness of theology as it sits uneasily in the contemporary academy. After all, the present intellectual context is hardly a naturally hospitable frame of reference for theology, and its practitioners must bear in mind the character of modernity, described by Rémi Brague as the 'retreat of the sacred'.[1] Theologians already work in a context of unsettled foundations and fractured presuppositions, and so a critical reading of both their own tradition and the practice of their discipline can create a healthy self-critical awareness.

To read Emmanuel Levinas is to be unsettled. His work unsettles philosophical orthodoxies and provokes the Western intellectual tradition at its foundations. That provocation is not the violence of one who shakes that tradition for the sake of it. He is not a vandal who destroys the work of his fathers or digs up the vineyard of his ancestors. On the contrary, Levinas learns a great deal from Plato and Aristotle, just as he is inspired by Husserl and, in turn, Heidegger. In the end, he saw himself as a philosopher just as they understood themselves to be philosophers. Even in his turn from Heidegger, Levinas invokes fundamental insights from the tradition so that his provocation might not be the stuff of vandalism and juvenile dismantling, but rather that of a mature judgement on the approach to Being. That judgement is both profound and staggering in its consequences. That is to say, it is a profoundly creative and interesting proposal as well as qualitatively far-ranging. For Levinas, Western philosophy has encumbered itself with an intransigent commitment to the category of Being to the detriment of the Other. The suffering other – the poor one, the widow, the orphan – is a subjective presence who appears before the self across a vast array of non-quantifiable difference. This difference is formed through the alterity of the other person who issues an ethical demand to one's own self that is, for Levinas, absolute.

Because Levinas' critique of philosophy is fundamentally far-reaching, theology cannot claim innocence of his charge. Theology falls within Levinas' sway as much as any other discipline. In fact, Levinas specifies theology as a problematic branch of thinking more than once. Because his claims continue to make their presence felt among a new generation of thinkers, theology owes to him an attentive attitude. We are invited to read his works carefully and open our theological concerns to the ethical questions Levinas generates. That does not mean a wholesale adoption of Levinas' thought; uncritical readings of Levinas will not do. It will be shown that theologians have argued for deficiencies in Levinas' phenomenological reading of the Other which carry a certain *gravitas*. Some of these are considered in the present work. Indeed, theology is a discourse with a long pedigree and is owed an attentive receptivity for its own resources in thinking through the challenge of Levinas. As Levinas opens up the possibility of describing the ethical relationship with an openness to the Other, theology rediscovers the alterity that provokes its own progress and renewal. To put it more markedly, theologians may read Levinas' accounts of the 'God' who comes to mind, and in turn become more acutely aware of the radical claims made in the God of 'revelation', to which their work is largely addressed. Theology may not only be re-formed through Levinas, but also be re-sourced and re-schooled by its masters.

Levinas is known as a French Jewish thinker, but his roots cannot be forgotten. He was born in Kaunas, Lithuania, a place besieged by the Nazis, the Communists and breathing freely once again in the confused liberties after the fall of the Berlin Wall. His birth date was 30 December 1905 according to the (then used) Julian Calendar, which falls on 12 January 1905 in the Gregorian usage. His youth took him to both Russia and back to Lithuania, before his relocation to the French university city of Strasbourg in 1923. In his traditional Jewish upbringing, he was called Emanuelis Levinas, later Westernized as Emmanuel Lévinas in his adoption of French citizenship and culture. According to biographer Saloman Malka, Levinas, along with his two younger brothers Boris and Aminadav, was privately tutored in Hebrew and practised an austere but not overly zealous religiosity; they attended synagogue, ate kosher and observed *Shabbat* and holy days.[2] In such a context, Levinas took to Russian literature (especially Pushkin, Dostoyevsky, Tolstoy and Gogol) and culture, without any diminishment of Judaism as a lived religion. Russian was his first language and it was spoken in his family home, but he took to others with enviable skill: German, English, Yiddish and French.

In looking briefly at Levinas' early life, it might be noted that Levinas disliked the 'pathos' of biographies. He held a certain disdain for the dramatic re-presentation of one's own life in the written word, for its necessary truncation of the complexities of a human life as it was lived and experienced, and had little patience for biographical discussions in interviews about his thought. Nevertheless, it remains informative to consider his personal history to a certain degree. The young Jewish Lithuanian, who was known to be intellectually gifted, linguistically accomplished and culturally well-mannered and hospitable, was the very image of educated middle-class aspiration. And it was the combination of these very gifts that took Levinas from his beloved Lithuanian homeland to France as a young man with dogged and joyful commitment. In 1928, having studied philosophy and giving himself to France ('It is Europe!'), Levinas travelled to Freiburg for the lectures of Edmund Husserl.[3] The father of phenomenology was by that stage in his later years and his younger student Martin Heidegger was filling lecture halls with enthusiastic devotees. Husserl's phenomenological method remained of great intrigue for many, but it lacked the urgency of new enquiry that Heidegger's *Being and Time* (1927) inspired. As Levinas put it, 'I went to Freiburg because of Husserl, but discovered Heidegger'.[4] Nevertheless, Levinas' brilliance was appreciated by both Husserl and Heidegger and he became a private guest and a respected visiting student, even at an early stage.

In 1930, Levinas became a French citizen and performed his duties in military service, as well as marrying Raïssa Levi, whom he had known since childhood. Although by this stage he had completed his license in philosophy, he took a teaching position at the Alliance Israélite Universelle in Paris rather than a university position. A number of essays appeared in print in the next few years, but none of them marked him as a radical or original thinker to the degree hailed by contemporaries like Jean-Paul Sartre. However, in 1935 his first thematic essay, 'On Escape' in *Recherches Philosophiques* appeared, representing an important witness to his attempt to break with Heidegger.[5] That same year his daughter was born and nothing of great consequence was published until much later.

The intervention of war brought great misfortune to Levinas' family. He was drafted into the French army as a translator in 1939 and taken prisoner of war in Rennes with the Tenth French Army in June 1940. For a number of months he was a captive in a Frontstalag before being transferred to a camp in Fallingpostel, not a great distance from Magdeburg in the German north. As an officer, Levinas was held in a military prisoner's camp rather than in a concentration camp, inducted into forced labour alongside his co-prisoners in camp number 1492. He often commented that this was the same number as the year in which the Jews were expelled from Spain. As a Jew, he was separated from non-Jewish prisoners and wore the insignia JUD on his uniform. As the years of the war went by, he was allowed limited correspondence with his wife, and he wrote much which was never completed. The trials of the period should not be underestimated, and in fact Levinas' wife and daughter were only saved by the intervention of friends including Maurice Blanchot, and the Religious Sisters of a Vincentian convent, as well as being provided for by a living allowance from Levinas' employers at the private school at which he taught, the École Normale Israélite Orientale (ENIO). Sadly, members of his family were murdered in the Nazi pogroms which began in the June of 1940, helped by the collaboration of some Lithuanian nationalists.[6]

With the end of the war in 1945, Levinas was released and he returned to Paris. Through the intervention of a friend, he was made the Director of the ENIO. His family remained in an apartment above the school until 1980 when they moved to another apartment in the same street. In Levinas' biography, there is a constant hint of a rich domesticity that disliked great interruption or change, a privacy which remained all the more mysterious by its hospitality to others. By all accounts, the Levinas marriage was a happy and contented one, hiding an interiority unreachable by those on the outside but insistent in its care and attention to visitors and friends. It was in this setting, after the war, that Levinas met Henri Nerson, a local doctor, and became his close friend. In turn, Nerson introduced Levinas to Monsieur Chouchani who became a teacher to the young philosopher (and now school administrator). Chouchani is the nickname for an otherwise anonymous rabbi who became a towering intellectual figure, greatly influencing a number of Jewish thinkers of that generation (e.g. Elie Wiesel). Chouchani spent time in Israel and Paris and died in Uruguay where his grave reads, '[t]he wise Rabbi Chouchani of blessed memory. His birth and his life are sealed in enigma'. His identity and biography is a contested topic, but Levinas admitted towards the end of his life that Chouchani had made a great impression upon him. It appears that Levinas and Nerson had taken to meeting with Chouchani weekly for Talmudic studies, despite the latter's description as dirty, unattractive and rather like a vagabond.

Earlier, in 1931, Levinas had co-translated Husserl's *Cartesian Meditations* into French with Gabrielle Pfeiffer, only 2 years after the completion of his doctorate on Husserl's theory of intuition. Indeed, his thesis had won a prize from the Institute of Philosophy and published by Vrin in 1930. Following the war, Levinas' career did not follow any classical or logical academic sequence, but there is no doubt that the experience of war, loss and bereavement marked Levinas interminably. As a teacher and administrator, Levinas' time was limited, but he retained a commitment to regular Talmudic reflections and written commentaries, as well as public meetings and smaller study groups. Between 1946 and 1947 Levinas gave a series of four lectures at the Collège Philosophique at the Sorbonne, which were subsequently published as *Time and the Other*.[7] We know from his Talmudic commentaries that Levinas continued to learn from his 'master', Monsieur Chouchani, with whom he studied between 1947 and 1949, and during which time it appears that the latter actually lived in Levinas' apartment.[8] In 1947, Levinas published the work he had written sporadically throughout the war, *Existence and Existents*.[9] This, in contrast to the existential works of his avant-garde contemporaries, considers existence as a preconscious phenomenological moment. Existence is not, in this work, to be equated simply with the existentiality of human experience, but as an event of understanding that sits unsettlingly before the human self. The self does not so much realize its existence in the world, but becomes aware of one's existence as a gift that is given before one may receive it. In the following years, a number of shorter works were published in addition to his ongoing Talmudic commentaries and an annual address to the *Colloque des intellectuels juifs de langue française*. These continued his rational and non-mystical readings of the Talmud and Scripture alongside political and social events of the day.

In 1961, Levinas published the first of his two major works, *Totality and Infinity*, which, alongside other shorter works, also served as his *doctorat d'état* thesis (the equivalent of the German habilitation thesis, which allows a doctored student to teach at university).[10] This altered Levinas' reception in the French academy in a significant way. In 1963, he published *Difficult Freedom*, his collection of shorter reflections on Jewish-related topics, and in 1964, he was appointed Professor of Philosophy at the University of Poitiers.[11] He remained the Director of the ENIO until 1980, despite his rapidly growing academic commitments. In 1967, Levinas became Professor of Philosophy at the new institution, University of Paris Nanterre. He gave two lectures there that were published in 1968 as 'Substitution', laying out the essential argument that unfolded in his second great work, *Otherwise than Being or Beyond Essence*, although this was not published until 1974.[12] In the intermediate 6 years, he published *Nine Talmudic Readings*, was awarded an honorary doctorate at Loyola University of Chicago (alongside Hannah Arendt), followed by the same honour at universities in Leiden, Holland (1975), Leuven, Belgium (1976), Fribourg, Switzerland

(1980) and Bar-Ilan, Isreal (1981).[13] In 1973, Levinas was made a Professor of Philosopher at the Sorbonne (Paris IV) and continued as an honorary professor after his retirement in 1976. Seminars were presented at the Sorbonne and elsewhere and other essays were gathered in collections in both French and English. The thought of *Otherwise than Being* is built on the radical philosophical departures of *Totality and Infinity* and it remains a question as to whether they constitute distinct arguments or variations on a single theme. Levinas' career is in no way a traditional or typical path. His commitment to Jewish-Christian relations, his regularity in Talmudic reflection and commentaries and his engaged philosophical development of a creative response to the work of Martin Heidegger open up Levinas' thought to interest from a range of perspectives. Theologically, there is a rich Levinasian heritage that is both provocative and demanding. In its provocation, it unsettles philosophical presuppositions and challenges theology. In its demand, Levinas' thought achieves a precognitive reflection; the thought of God spontaneously arises once again before the mental horizon and challenges thought in the midst of other people and the infinity present in the face.

The provocation of Levinas cannot be viewed clearly without these biographical details, constituting the basis for some reflection upon his thought. Levinas is rightly understood as a Jewish thinker, but here it must be said that there is argument among Jewish philosophers as to how one might relate the religion to the man in question. Because so much of Levinas' work is grappling with Heidegger's 'being-towards-death', the subject of death is referred to repeatedly, and not as an abstracted concept. In both Heidegger and Levinas, the problem of death is a uniquely human subject. It stands at a convergence of human existentiality as an insurmountable and unavoidable givenness. As each person lives, so each must also die. Its experience is unavoidable, yet human philosophizing remains the activity of the living. There is no testimony from those beyond the grave as such, and so words remain the constructs of anticipation and not of knowledge itself. Furthermore, death is both the universal problem and the intrinsically personal event that may only be experienced individually. Only the oneself can experience one's own death. And having died, the oneself has no voice with which to give testimony to it. Levinas rejects Heidegger's insistence that *Dasein*'s authenticity is achieved in its living towards death. Instead, Levinas proposes that it is the death of the Other that interrupts one's in-authenticity and makes possible one's own living towards and for the Other.

These general contours of a life lived against the backdrop of war and death shape the thought of Emmanuel Levinas. They inform it and they provide a means by which his thought can be addressed without abstraction from the world in memory and history. And moreover, they allow an entry point into the pervading provocation of the two major works of Levinas, *Totality and Infinity* and *Otherwise than Being: or Beyond Essence*. In both, Levinas unsettles the course of thinking in the category of 'Being', which opens up upon a significant point of both fruitfulness, and contestability, between theology and philosophy.

Chapter 2

Being's Other

Two major works of Levinas, *Totality and Infinity* [Totalité et infini: essai sur l'extériorité] and *Otherwise than Being: or Beyond Essence* [Autrement qu'être ou au-delà de l'essence], are examples of some of the most imaginative and rigorous radical philosophy of the twentieth century. Together they constitute a large-scale critique of Western philosophy in its traditional permutations, and respond specifically to major thinkers of the modern era, including René Descartes, Edmund Husserl and Martin Heidegger. Levinas' critique is essentially ethical; that philosophy has bound itself to a Greek notion of Being to the detriment of otherness. That is to say, in the category of Being, the difference that marks one person from another is annulled and the unique otherness of the individual is lost. Worse than this, the very alterity of the other person is subjugated under the impositions of ontology. For Levinas, this is intrinsically unethical, because it substitutes categories of ontology and essence for the alterity of the other person. Levinas argues that the totalization evident in categories of Being obliterates the Other, whereas attention to the event of alterity reveals the infinity of the Other. In this way, Levinas does not dismantle Being as such, but takes leave of it as the central philosophical category, re-constituting what he calls the Other as the key event for philosophical reflection.[1] Levinas offers a philosophy cognizant of the Heideggerian distinction between being (*da-sein*) and beings (*das Seiende*), referred to as Heidegger's 'ontological difference', but accentuates the significance of the other person in the social experience of *da-sein*; an experience Levinas views as the 'infinity which opens in the ethical relationship of man to man'.[2]

In the event of the Other, Levinas identifies a structure of inter-subjectivity that phenomenology may interrogate with startling new insights. Ultimately, he concludes that in the epiphany of alterity, the other person issues a demand that the oneself acts with an absolute responsibility, resulting in an asymmetrical structure of call and response. Levinas' work on the I–Other dynamic has been a major influence on figures such as Jacque Derrida, Jean-Luc Marion and Jean-Yves Lacoste. Also, throughout his work, Levinas develops points of dialogue with a range of other major voices, such as Maurice Blanchot, Paul Ricœur and John Paul II. While this chapter deals with the major themes of *Totality and Infinity* and *Otherwise than Being*, this book argues that examples of the most fruitful moments of Levinas' corpus appear in other works, including essays and Talmudic commentaries. Nevertheless, none of these texts – essays and interviews, along with shorter books – can be understood without an account of Levinas' two largest monographs, which in fact would be enough on their own to constitute Levinas as one of the few original thinkers.

The first of these books, *Totality and Infinity*, was published in 1961 and marks a crucial stage in Levinas' wider intellectual reception. It is his attempt to respond to the weaknesses in both his great mentors, Edmund Husserl and Martin Heidegger, and to assert an alternative to what he perceives to be the dominant Western philosophical model. For Levinas, that model is deeply problematic because of its obsession with ontology, which is a totalizing tendency that denies the infinity of the other person. Indeed, the other person – the *Other* – represents the pivot point on which Levinas' philosophy turns; that of the supremacy of care and responsibility that issues from the face of the other person and provokes the self to action. Such a responsibility offers a moral content that hushes the clamouring urgency of politics and competing cultural practices. Levinas opens his preface with the claim, 'it is of the highest importance to know whether we are not duped by morality'.[3] The very idea that the prevailing culture might have been fooled by a moral façade (the French 'morale' could also be rendered, in this context, as 'morals') that lacks truth or authenticity should be frightening. It is a question that, if answered in the alternative, requires a re-evaluation of social approaches to other people across thought, institutions, relationships and politics. Levinas unpacks his challenge by viewing war as the great confrontation with morality, and it, in turn, as an ordeal that renders morality derisory. Behind war lies politics, which is the exercise of reason.[4] The travesty of war then is twofold: It is the material exercise of reason in its absolute guise, and it is the destruction of individuals, not simply through death, but as the domination of their otherness or their difference. The violence of war is rendered possible by the Western philosophical exercise of its understanding of reason, and so Being becomes a bloody denial of alterity. Reason, in the example of war, describes others as mere obstacles to one's political aspirations, and processes, means and categories by which they may be annihilated or subjugated. In the prescience of Levinas' description, there can be seen the essential argument which unfolds at length throughout *Totality and Infinity*. The graphic connection between reason and war, and the insistent conflict between politics and morality, provides a picture of sociality interrogated philosophically by Levinas. In untangling the philosophical knot that has been tied between war, politics and morality, Levinas opens up a new way of reasoning, one that in fact reasons against the very category of reason that results in the priority of ontology.

So, where does Levinas locate the point at which such a new way of reasoning can begin? The answer is not simply in the category of alterity, as if that alone would suffice, but in the *epiphany* of alterity, in the event of its appearing. This event, for Levinas, is located in the face [*visage*] of 'the Other' [*autrui*].[5] In the face, transcendence gleams, thus constituting an infinity of meaning and possibility. In the face of the Other, subjectivity becomes a contextualization through which the other person is conceived as one who provokes a response; an infinity that exceeds the otherness of the Other and demands of the oneself some level of return, much like an answer to a call or, perhaps better, a summons. Subjectivity is then an intrinsic hospitality to other persons. It is a construal of human being that does not deny otherness but instead receives it as an ethical obligation of care, and of a consciousness that does not limit itself to what is describable or containable. Chiefly, this localizing of responsibility in the infinity of the face of the Other is reached by way of phenomenology, which for Levinas is the 'intentional analysis' that remains the 'search for the concrete'.[6] While Levinas makes reference to the influence of Franz Rosenzwieg's *Stern der Erlösung* [The Star of Redemption], he describes phenomenological method as offering the basic structure for his ensuing argument.[7] Phenomenology opens up the experience of the world to the exercise of authentic examination, of the substance of events and things as they appear to one's consciousness. The analogy of vision is important to Levinas' phenomenology, in which the face of the Other appears and is witnessed. For him, ethics is an 'optics', a means of witnessing and then acting in response to the appearance of alterity in the face.[8] One not only hears or observes the Other, but also witnesses the event of alterity in the face of the Other. Another way of putting it is to say that the face must be experienced by the self, and therefore troubled and awakened to the good of the other person. The face of the Other is an exteriorization of a personal non-reducibility that interrupts the oneself and issues a demand for an ethical response. The face not only appears, but also makes itself appear as a witness to its own need. It could be said that the face discloses responsibility, but for Levinas, it never discloses its own self, which remains absolutely Other. This problem will be addressed further.

Now, the description of the face not only elicits the provocation to act ethically, but also arouses a desire. This is what Levinas calls 'metaphysical desire'.[9] By this term, he upholds the tradition of an invisible trajectory experienced by the human subject, which settles upon a beyond or an otherwise that sits outside of what is immediately at hand in the world. Yet he develops a particular interpretation of metaphysical desire. Levinas writes, at the beginning of the first section of *Totality and Infinity*, that the 'true life is absent', and that, despite our desire for something totally beyond, human beings find themselves oriented or turned towards a something which is beyond the world and, yet, remains in the world: 'But we are in the world'.[10] This is the incarnate quandary that Levinas' philosophy seeks to address, that of the juxtaposition of the human person whose desire is metaphysical, and yet whose situation is grounded in a material and concrete situation. While Levinas maintains that metaphysical desire is an authentically experienced phenomenon, he defines it apart from the notion of need. Desire and need are distinguished profoundly.

In 'desire', one's hope for a heightened otherness that sits out of reach is urgent and invisible, bringing one close to terms such as death or goodness in a heightened disinterest and noble sense. In 'need', the person does not experience a metaphysical directionality, but rather the coring out of the self in the hope that a hole will be filled or a hunger met. The experience of needfulness is a 'less' which can be satisfied.[11] One might think of the distinction in terms of one's own experience. The self might have missed breakfast, and as the hours pass by, a needful hunger develops within the physiological dimensions of the body. The stomach growls and the mind feels unable to concentrate on mundane tasks. Creativity is short-lived and the body experiences a need, settling upon the objective of a lunchtime meal as its only satiation. And so one's imagination crafts the means by which that meal will be obtained; perhaps a particular restaurant or café and the fastest route to follow. However, at other times, the self feels a restlessness of spirit in search for something transcendent to immediate experience. Its hunger and thirst may have been met, or any number of objectives reached, and there remains an *as yet*, a longing for something more within the challenges and discourses of life. The need/desire distinction is a crucial piece in the Levinasian puzzle, for it links together the metaphysical nature of alterity with its embodied and subjective experience in human living. The human person experiences the distinction not as an exceptional aspect of human life, but as a basic and integral aspect of typical human experience. This illustrates the distance that a human being has from the world, and an uprootedness that disconnects the embodied human subject from the objective meeting of its most basic requirements, because need and desire often infringe on each other and we cannot distinguish them clearly in our day-to-day choices. Needful objectives are 'dependencies' upon the world revealed in being cold, hungry, thirsty, naked or in search for shelter, and furthermore, they clarify the way in which a person overcomes a dependant distance in the world.[12] While needfulness shows how much the human body requires the otherness of the world to meet it in satiation, it is also a self-possession or self-governance that can overcome the world. The human person knows it is hungry, and becomes aware that it has some power to meet its need and to overcome the destitution of the world. While the need for a meal is great, it is also the opportunity to recognize that needfulness does not govern human action. It provokes, challenges and demeans it at different intervals, but through it the rational human animal exercises a freedom in how it manages that need.

Nevertheless, the satiation of need is a world away from the possibility of meeting the hopes of metaphysical desire. In need, one can embrace the being of the world in some tangible presence and assimilate its otherness into the self. Levinas writes of sinking one's teeth 'into the real' and finding satisfaction.[13] Food can fill the stomach. Water can quench the tongue. A sexual liaison can gratify the body's natural appetite. But for Levinas, need's fulfilment in the being of the world inculcates the event of time into its basic mechanism. Time is available to the oneself as the space in which need can be met in the world;

one is presupposed by another in the order of time. Without time, need has no room to manoeuvre towards what it longs for and conduct the assimilation Levinas describes. Where does this time come from? For Levinas, time is available because desire comes *before* need. That is to say, metaphysical desire is a directionality that is intrinsic to the transcendent nature of the human person, who is able to perceive and adjust its relationship with the alterity of the world. Before we are hungry, we are restless for transcendence. Because human persons are desiring creatures who inherently hope for an invisible objective beyond the world, time can be viewed as a kind of gift in which the more animalistic category of need can be met. Desire gives time to the self, which makes available the satiation of need. As a bodily form of existence, the human being discovers that desire opens towards that which flesh and blood cannot meet, the 'unchartered future' which moves upwards towards the height of an alterity that is both distant and encountered in its transcendence.[14]

In the distinction between need and desire, it can be seen that Levinas' account of what the human person hopes for is an important means of assessing Levinas' philosophy. His account of Being is one in which ontology is not the first category, but rather that of alterity. In otherness, humans encounter that which speaks from a beyond, thus raising the spectre of metaphysical desire in an en-fleshed moment. In other words: the face-to-face event of experiencing the presence of the other person. This theme is explored further in Levinas' second major work.

In *Otherwise than Being: or Beyond Essence*, Levinas develops themes present in *Totality and Infinity* and delves deeper into his recasting of Being in terms of alterity. It is a book devoted to the memory of those people who were 'closest among the six million assassinated by the National Socialists' and countless others who have been made victims of 'the same hatred of the other man, the same anti-semitism'.[15] Following the dedication is a second, this time in Hebrew, which lists

Levinas' father, mother, brother, father-in-law and mother-in-law. As Hilary Putnam has observed, the connection between Levinas' close family members and all who have become victims because of otherness or difference is striking.[16] In Putnam's view, the anti-Semitism that Levinas describes is the rejection of all who are different, and not only those Jews who suffered directly because of their Jewishness. One can think of those outside the Jewish fold who suffered and died in the Holocaust, including homosexuals, Jehovah's Witnesses, artists and Christians. The burden of *Otherwise than Being* is not only to describe the role of difference, but also to think otherwise than the metaphysics traditionally practised in Western thought. Of course, the implication of this association of metaphysics with the Holocaust is the striking critique that a false philosophy bears some role in the sufferings of the Shoah. This cannot be decisively proven or disproven, but Levinas' implication is present in all of his major works, and falls heavily on the notion that ethical responsibility is issued directly from the face-to-face moment of self-disclosure.

As Graham Ward has argued, a similar plot is developed in *Totality and Infinity* and *Otherwise than Being*.[17] In both, and evidenced in other texts such as *Time and the Other*, is the explication of the primacy of the Other [*autrui*] who draws the self out in an act of responsibility.[18] The seductive nature of this drawing out is constructed textually. For both Levinas' longer philosophical works and his other shorter books and essays, the words build up a provocation that entices the reader into the narrative. For Ward, those texts are essentially 'performative', inviting readers into a plot as it penetrates more deeply within its own insistent logic.[19] That logic opens in *Otherwise than Being* as a description of the problem of Being and of essence.[20] For Levinas, essence, or the event of Being – *esse* – is not the particularized concretization of the individual being (e.g. the human *being*), but of the inscription in theorized language and thought forms of an idea for ontology that sits trenchant in Western thought; pervasive, restrictive and recurring. It is an entrenched rejection of what Ward calls the 'narrative of the other', which exposes the dislocation of alterity by a privileging of Being.[21] Ward emphasizes also the way in which Levinas' texts do not restrict themselves to constructing a philosophy, but of drawing the reader in to participate in a new way of thinking. The implication of such an approach is directed towards the pressing requirement for ethical action in the limited field of experience in which the human person lives in history.

The primacy of the Other, as Levinas poetically encircles his subject, is a provocation to act; it cannot be limited to an intellectual argument or assignation of theory and ideas. The seduction of the reader who engages with Levinas' writing is enacted as an awakening to a presence that is always present and never without a need of its own. The text raises one's eyes to the needful Other and convicts the self with the responsibility of caring thoughtfully for the welfare of the Other. Levinas' provocation is not one of moral outrage or the cry of the prophet, but of the philosopher's lament; the descriptive analysis of a thinker who observes in incarnate existence an ethical demand overlooked by others. Because of the poetic rendering of Levinas' words, this lament is all the more enticing in its seductive pull, even as its demand seems impossible to meet in any normative quantifiable measure.

So, in this linguistic demand of responsibility, how does *Otherwise than Being* entice the reader? It puts forward a suggestive philosophical outline that centres upon the presence of the other person and not on a formal argument as such. Levinas builds in *Otherwise than Being* an appeal that relies on phenomenological language not bound by the formal categories defined by Husserl. For example, the classic formulation of the phenomenological reduction – the *epoché* – in which the world is bracketed out of a particular objective study, is only partially maintained. In the sixth Cartesian meditation, Husserl developed further a theme that had been growing since his early works, that of a process by which one can decaptivate one's intentional analysis from the world.[22] In bracketing out the world, one intends a pure consciousness towards the object of one's study, and so the objective content of what appears is evident on its own terms. The *epoché* is an illustration of Husserl's later transcendental turn, but readers of his work can detect its origins in his earliest writings. Levinas' phenomenological reduction relies on the same basic notion, but extends a complication in its practice. For Levinas, the essential analysis does involve an authentic encounter with the object at hand, but by its own logic, the object itself expresses a reverse intentionality in the process of analysis. In the case of the human subject, intentionality is inverted such that the objective presence of another effects a reverse gaze upon the one who first gazes (to use an imprecise optical metaphor). In stripping back the world, the full content of a subjective world that inhabits the otherness of the Other stares back at the self and intends not a strict science of discovery, but what Levinas calls an ethical subjectivity. In this way, the self becomes not the active gazer, but a strict passivity before the intentionality of alterity. For Levinas, this passivity can be described as a 'pure saying itself', and an event that strips the self of its sovereignty and active subjectivity.[23] The enticement spoken of above is not conducted in an easy comfort among friends, but of a provocative demand that convicts the self before the Other. For Leslie Macavoy, the inversion of Husserl's intentionality is a switching of the poles between the intender and the receiver of the intentional gaze and constitutes more an enigma than a phenomenon.[24] This is a helpful description, because the content of this reduction is an experience that remains mysterious, even in Levinas' own account. Yet it is profoundly subjective, in that the stripping of the world reveals two subjects in an intense ethical relationship. It is a reverse intentionality immersed in a moral significance that remains always intentional, and one experienced in human subjectivity. The human subject receives from its human counterpart an assignation of localized ethical responsibility. Realization of this can be unnerving, rather like sensing that a stranger is staring at oneself in a darkened room.

Who are they? What is their intention? How can one protect oneself? But in the darkness, none of these questions have an answer, for no means of answering the questions are at hand. One must find or wait for the light. And the voice of the Other must be waited upon as a troubling exercise of otherness, even while it remains unknown whether the voice is one person only, or merely one among a crowd.

Now, the typical means of assessing this problem is to discover who or what the Other is. To extend the simile further, one's natural inclination is to learn about the other person, either by direct communication or subterfuge. Who is this person in *my* room? In what way are they a threat to *me*? Perhaps the darkened room is one's own lounge room, and the perception of a trespasser has been noted before switching on the light. For Levinas, the question of who or what the Other is becomes an illegitimate question. This is the ontological question. It is not driven by an authentic interest in the other party, but by the subjective longing to protect oneself from a possible threat. One wants to protect one's own flesh and blood, as it were, and to keep safe what belongs to the self. Being driven by the fear of loss is hardly a merciful responsibility for the other person, even if one's desire for safety is altogether warranted. The more appropriate question for Levinas is that of asking how might the self respond to the Other. Levinas does not use the image, but if Western philosophy is the dark room of which one speaks, Levinas' analysis is such that one waits passively for the other to switch the light on and reveal himself or herself. And in that flooding revelation of optical clarity, the other is seen, present and waiting.

Alterity becomes not the threat perceived by the self in one's horrified imagination, but of the needfulness inherent in the face of the other person. There before the self is a frail structure of human longing and subjective need. The other person is poor and spiritually malnourished. In the dark, the Other has not revealed its sex, skin colour, ethnicity or age. There in the dark of one's own home, the Other intrudes as a needful person before any other personal traits have been revealed. Before this particular Other, the self becomes unsettled and provoked in responsibility. Suddenly, the homeless man on the street, or the hungry child in a foreign land, or the lonely widow at death's door is in *my* home and facing me with need written across the face. This is the unsettling moment that Levinas takes from his phenomenological analysis of the event of inter-subjectivity. One begins to find in Levinas' writings the counter-intuitive suggestion that one is *already* in a darkened room and one is *already* faced with an anxious responsibility for the other person. Such a suggestion is disturbingly intimate in its association of strangeness in the face of the Other with one's own conflicted ethical responsibility.

The result of such a conviction is of a de-centred subjectivity. While Levinas maintains that the self, or the human subject, remains an 'irreplaceable uniqueness', he also views an existential unsettling of the self in its exposure to alterity.[25] He calls this a de-posing or de-situating of the subject. In this way, it cannot be argued that Levinas' turn to the subject carries the same level of self-infatuation evident in contemporary popular culture. This is not the overanalysed means of reinventing the self without regard for questions of transcendence or ethics that one might find on the glossy covers of magazines or television commercials. Levinas' turn to the subject is a troubling exercise that denies a model of subjectivity that privileges categories like self-determination or self-autonomy. Indeed, it is the abolition of personal sovereignty in so far as one perceives one's relationship to other persons. This abolishment is issued on behalf of the other person as the Other, and defines one's unsettling ethical responsibility on the grounds of an alterity that is absolute. Although Levinas achieves this alongside his various comments that uniqueness is not denied, some have argued that this relationship is tendentious. After all, Levinas' account of the Other is itself the frame in which the self finds its ethical vocation; it always relies on alterity as an infinity of significance. For Joeri Schrijvers, Levinas' account can be critiqued by a certain reading of Heidegger, in which being-with-others is always enacted in a limited and determinate circle of others.[26] What seemed obvious for Heidegger is that one's own subjectivity always follows a certain belonging within the world, such that the Other is met within the determinate circle. This maintains a meeting of the face-to-face, but without the Levinasian rendering of alterity in an absolute sense. For Schrijvers, the local and particularized other person is still a radical departure for a robust philosophy, but in this way a certain uniqueness of the Other is maintained. One could then suggest that transcendence remains a possibility, even as an authentic immanence is given its due attention. As Schrijvers argues:

> Transcendence would be meaningful only *through*
> and *in* immanence. Instead of a negative appraisal of
> particularity, we perhaps need to learn to value this
> immanent opening to otherness otherwise.[27]

The two – transcendence and immanence – work as means of assessing responsibility for the particular Other. One does not infringe upon the Other but receives from the unique constellation of the incarnate Other's face and person the character of a personalized alterity. An otherness is present that still unsettles in a dark room, as it were, and requires the attention of the self. Even as one is awake within the dark room, one becomes acutely aware of a heightened sensory awareness when one perceives the presence of a stranger. One listens, looks and reacts in a more intently attentive mood. The question is whether the de-centring of subjectivity provokes the responsible self adequately.

In the account of alterity in *Totality and Infinity* and its development towards a richer notion of sensibility in *Otherwise than Being*, Levinas outlines an 'Other' whose alterity is austere. It is a subjectively experienced otherness within the inter-subjective moment itself, but without the complications of human sociality in its incarnate experience. That is not to say that Levinas denies incarnate existence, but it remains a problematic area of his thought that will be studied elsewhere in this book. Here, it is enough to emphasize the absence of incarnate life as a means of conveying personal responsibility in Levinas' major works. Certainly, he refers to incarnate existence, but he does not view it as a source for the absolute trajectory his ethical thought otherwise follows. For example, he refers to breathing as 'opening up'; to the 'non-alienation' of the giving of the body; the phenomenal importance of the 'sensible'; and even maternity as 'being par excellence'.[28] These are moments of sincere incarnate human experience, and of the event of Being as a presence that elicits a response. It is the call of the flesh that reverberates in the event of being one's own body. Levinas confirms these moments as being of phenomenological importance, and seems to indicate subtle trajectories by which his thought may extricate from incarnate existence some truths that remain hidden from the eyes of the non-critical. And yet, Levinas, when alighting upon human flesh in its experienced signification, will say: 'The tenderness of skin is the very gap between approach and approached, a disparity, a non-intentionality, a non-teleology'.[29] Such disparity is of the space between that which is experienced and that which eludes experience in the exchange with the other person. The infinity of the Other is neither caught in the act of saying nor by any other thesis or category, and in fact refuses every incarnate presence.[30]

In Chapter 2, this problem is explored from a theological perspective with reference to St Athanasius. Here, it is viewed as a problem that contemporary theology both recognizes, while also needing to face with greater clarity. The work of Jean-Luc Marion is an important example of thought that crosses the divide between philosophy and theology, and owes much to a critical reading of Levinas. For Marion, an important positive contribution from Levinas is the discovery of the inversion of intentionality between the sender and the receiver.[31] In the reversal of the two poles, Levinas identifies the ethical moment *par excellence*, as described above. The strict intentionality that Husserl constructs in his phenomenological description is, on close inspection, merely a movement along the way towards its own intense reversal. It is not a turning about so much as it is a thoroughgoing inversion of the self in the content of the gaze. Marion takes from the Levinasian inversion a kind of counter-consciousness that the latter views as crucial to his philosophy. The immensity of the Other's ethical demand turns one's mind back upon itself as an elected servant of the other person's need. This notion of election is not for Marion the complete story. He turns to the language of the gift and the gifted to describe the particularly experienced call to act for the Other.[32] Whereas Levinas' account views incarnate existence as ultimately non-describable (the other is always *the* Other), Marion holds that the particular and fleshly moment of the face-to-face remains both other and intrinsic to ethical responsibility. He argues that the call of the face is both an imposition to respond *for* him and *to* him.[33] The call of the Other certainly remains the event of alterity in the sense of otherness demanding an ethical responsibility. But it is also a visible rendering of that same otherness, so that the demand overcomes every intuition to centred subjectivity and breaks the self apart from such intuitions. The Other de-centres the self and appeals directly from a localized incarnate presence.

In the event of the subject's de-centred call, Marion holds in tension the relationship between an other as always authentically other, with the localized incarnate presence that Levinas inconsistently de-values. However, Marion is concerned not simply with inter-subjectivity in its strictly human dimension, but in a phenomenological description of multiple moments in which alterity meets the self and saturates one's intuitive gaze. Marion calls this, 'saturated phenomena', and it illustrates a theological direction in which Levinas' thought might be taken.[34] The phenomenological description of certain events as marked chiefly by an excessive quality in the act of reception and experience goes beyond what most phenomenologists would account as respectable or traditional phenomenology as such. What is important to the present discussion is the way in which Marion relies on Levinas' reversal of the two poles (the giver and the receiver) as the basis upon which he follows the intentional gaze as far. In doing so, Marion relies on Levinas and also departs further from him. He finds in intentionality a movement that is ultimately inverted and, in certain circumstances, floods and overcompensates its own presence within the register of subjective intuition. He identifies the following phenomena as meeting this description: the event, the idol, the flesh and the icon.[35] Furthermore, Marion argues that within the final topic – that of the icon – one can find enfolded each of the previous three, thus showing that saturated phenomena do not give themselves within the same degree of givenness.[36]

A brief description of each is helpful. In the event, Marion specifies historical phenomenon such as particular events or epochs, in which the sheer quantity of perspectives and experiences saturates our own intuitional capacity to recognize and describe the event. For example, in the battle of Waterloo, Marion writes of each unique perspective as itself unable to encompass the event, despite each being an intrinsic subjective experience of that event. Neither soldier nor Emperor saw all that occurred and as such, the transmission of the historical event constitutes a proliferation of horizons, all of which are valid in themselves, but exceeded by the plurality of others.

In the idol, Marion notes a paradox in which one's intuition surpasses the conceptual whole of a given object, most notably in the example of the picture before one's eyes. The *givenness* of the idol is such that the receiver or gazer must enter a sequence of gazes in which one's own person is mirrored in each reflective moment. Even habits of seeing and conceptualizing what one witnesses in the image cannot limit the picture to a certain description or categorization. It is received again and again as a conceptual whole that must be reinterpreted and re-evaluated. Unlike the event, the idol can only ever foster this particularly solipsistic intentionality. One interprets one's own interpretative relationship to the picture with each gaze, and so the idol speaks ultimately not of its own meaning, but of the self-inferred meaning which opens up from within the human subject.

In the flesh, Marion notes the third type of saturated phenomenon. Here, he defines flesh as the 'identity of what touches with the medium where this touching takes place'.[37] He views this in an absolute sense, by which the flesh is a receptive form in that it passively bears the intuitive impressions of that which touches it, both real and derived. The flesh is both passive and strangely auto-affective, achieving such a status because it is not affective by any other substantive movement or event. It feels each affective moment by virtue of itself, whether in agony or joy, or any other. The self-affectivity experienced in the flesh is motivated only by itself in a certain localized immanence. Two points are important for Marion regarding the flesh. First, in contrast to the idol but similar to the event, it cannot be seen. That is, the auto-affection of the flesh occurs in an immediacy that is experienced by its own inhabitants and not in the gaze of others. Second, unlike the event, and in relation to its non-visibility, the flesh cannot be experienced by others. It is ultimately *mine*. It shows itself not by appearing but by its experience. In its 'mineness', the flesh is a self-giving that saturates one's own intuition. Before being seen, and because it cannot be seen, the flesh is experienced in the subjective moment as a giving-over of itself to the self. And in doing so, it 'gives me to myself'.[38]

In the final phenomenon, that of the icon, the intentional gaze is situated first in a unidirectionality that occurs outside the self. The icon is the intense gazer that admits of no reversal in the movement of intentionality; and moreover does not even constitute a site to be seen or a spectacle to be witnessed. It is an auto-manifestation that cannot be witnessed, because its whole eventfulness is constituted upon its own terms and not on that of the subject who receives this act of being gazed upon. At this point, Marion explicitly takes up the notion of the Other in Levinasian terms. The Other gazes at the self. There is nothing to see in the Other, for in an absolute otherness a gaze foists itself hard upon one's own receptive posture and 'gives itself only to be endured'.[39] Like Levinas, Marion finds in this reversal of intentionality an essentially ethical content that seems at times unbearable. The ardour of the Other sits wildly in the gaze, exceeding any capacity to circumvent the signification of the Other by one's own intentional gaze. No, the latter is denied, and as such, situates the presence of the Other as the constitution of the self, thus enabling the process of de-centring subjectivity described above. The Other-as-icon constitutes both an important phenomenological stage in itself and marking Marion's own thought as a unique intersection of theological and philosophical investigation. In the iconic status of the Other, Marion notes the characteristics of each of his other four topics of saturated phenomena. Like the historical event, multiple horizons and narrations cross over one another in meaning and significance, opening the icon up to a teleology. Like the idol, the icon draws one's attention towards it and seeks out an audience. It wants the subject to look upon it, even though its content cannot be witnessed. It exercises what Marion calls an individuation over the gaze that confronts it with the fullness of a demand. And like the flesh, the icon brings about an affect within the self that comes close to auto-affection. The icon seems to gather up these other phenomenon and confirm the legitimacy of Marion's discovery of the saturated phenomena, while also revealing a new threshold by which otherness can be described according to the basic criteria outlined by Levinas.

Across all four phenomena is the fact of givenness. Each arrives as a givenness manifested upon its own terms and which in turn denies every attempt to limit to descriptive categories of thought and argumentation. Traditional philosophy cannot contain these events; they are given to excess. In particular, the icon reveals a way of taking up Levinas' inversion of the two poles – receiver and gazer – and seeing in it the possibility of a phenomenon of revelation. Marion maintains that while phenomenology opens up a way to describe the meaning and significance of the event of revelation, what it cannot achieve is a decisive comment upon whether revelation 'can or should ever give itself'.[40] That is, Marion views phenomenology as a fruitful exercise in bracketing out the world and discovering a thing upon its own terms, but on the topic of revelation, phenomenology cannot confirm or deny the possibility or impossibility of the existence of the thing in question. Here, it might be said that phenomenology shows itself as a philosophical endeavour that is neither closed to theological reflection nor certain about its possibility.

Now, keeping in mind Marion's limitation and openness for revelation within the thought forms of phenomenology, he does insist that should revelation be an actual phenomenon, it would assume the figure of what he calls the 'paradox of paradoxes'. This relies primarily on the non–existence of any prerequisite condition or conditions upon which an event is determined in intentionality. In other words, the Other appears of its own accord, not upon any prior conviction, thought or determination. It will be a phenomenon that assimilates impossibility into its possibility and offers itself as a saturated phenomenon. What shows itself appears only as what gives itself. And as such, it appears only as the given. For Marion, revelation, therefore, is constituted within an eventfulness characterized by all four examples: the event, the idol, the flesh and the icon. To be more exact, revelation is iconic and therefore exacting the characters also of the event, the idol and the flesh. One must remember that Marion is not describing revelation *qua* revelation, but phenomenologically exploring the category of revelation as a possibility. Even to do this is a radical move within contemporary thought, for it opens philosophy's door to theology, not by an inch, but as far as it may be turned. As the paradox of paradoxes, revelation is not only iconic, but also exacting in its intentionality towards the receiver. It is the gaze above all gazes, and the intentionality that exceeds every intuition. For Marion, this is a philosophical observation that he makes, while attempting to respect the line between philosophy and what he calls 'revealed' theology.[41]

On this Levinasian basis, Marion determines in Jesus Christ the paradox of paradoxes and of the iconic event that saturates the intuitive gaze par excellence. Christ appears as an event, and as idol and as flesh. The coming of Christ, foretold by prophecy and fulfilled before human eyes, carries Christ forward as a historical narrative and, uniquely, as an epoch embodied in the life of one man. The idolatrous nature of Christ's appearing lies in the way all human reflections upon him must face their own self-conceits and obsessions. The human person cannot help but appraise himself in Christ, and with all the gusto of false pride, find in him an affirmation of personal hopes and desires. But of course deeper reflection finds that in the flesh of Christ, one stands before an icon who looks upon the self. Marion calls upon a number of scriptural references to support his appraisal of Christ as the characterization of each of these expressions of the saturated phenomena. One is worth recalling. In John 18:6-7, Christ names himself: 'It is me (I am)'.[42] This moment, in which the betrayer Judas brings forth a band of soldiers armed with weapons and torches, reveals the excessive nature of Christ's presence before others. In the light shining in the hands of his enemies, and in full knowledge of their interior dispositions towards him, Christ does not name them but himself. He reveals his own interiority which is greater than that of his violent interlocutors. Jesus asks them who they seek and they answer, 'Jesus of Nazareth'. Upon answering in the affirmative, 'I am he', men of strength and skill, 'drew back and fell to the ground'. Marion links this small but significant moment to the later resurrection, and in both events the paradox of Christ 'passes beyond what this world can receive, contain, or embrace'.[43] Jesus the Christ is a figure presented in the narrative as indeed the paradox of paradoxes;

of an immensity of divine presence that sits beyond Being itself, outside the world and all the world can contain in fact and in perception. Yet he stands before human eyes and speaks words that strike the human heart with an authentic and weighty presence. At times his presence is unbearable, causing the swift fall-back of his enemies. At other times, it draws his interlocutors into his own heart and reveals depths that move also beyond the world and its limitations. Indeed, the world turns against Christ because it cannot contain or perceive him. This is what Marion calls 'common-law phenomenology', the investigation of inherently quotidian worldly events without regard (and therefore leading to violent rejection) for the possibility of revelation. Marion turns to the structure of the New Testament itself, in which it takes four Gospel writers to tell Christ's narrative, and even then admitting to severe limits in what they tell of the event of Jesus of Nazareth. (See John 21:25, in which the author wonders whether the world could contain all the books that might tell Jesus' many wonders.)

This example of a theological interpretation of Levinas' appeal to alterity is important because it places its accent upon a God who is revealed in the events of human subjectivity. As the paradox of paradoxes, Christ appears as a phenomenon that not only takes up the four types of paradox – the saturated phenomenon – but also redoubles the saturation that defines that of the icon. By redoubling, Marion indicates two things. First, that the gaze of the icon establishes the subject itself. See for example the rich young man in Mark 10:17-22. Here, the paradox of Christ 'gazed upon and loved' the man, constituting him as the beloved and assigning him as the particular object of affection. Christ does not simply cast his gaze, but gazes upon the man with a profound degree of specificity. As such, Marion views such a gaze as marking the man as a witness to that which gazes upon the man to begin with. Second, the saturated phenomenon of Christ redoubles his own phenomenality elsewhere upon the poor and those who the man is commanded to love. He is told to sell his goods and give them to the poor. Christ's own saturated gaze is given over, as it were, to others, allowing them to stand in his place and proffer upon the rich young man the same intense gaze of ethical responsibility. This redoubling of the paradox of paradoxes is what Marion calls 'saturation to the second degree'.[44] It is a saturation that, in itself, gives itself over even as an excess. But not as an excess that overruns a cup and disappears into the crevices and gaps of the path at one's feet, but as one that manifests itself concretely in the faces of the poor and those in need, thus redoubling paradoxically in a phenomenality that may be witnessed, loved and attended to.

And so, Levinas' purchase on alterity opens a way to interpret the event of Christ with a fresh perspective, without disregarding the significance of human relationships. Marion's descriptions of Christ as revelation *par excellence*, and as revelation open to phenomenological enquiry, are crucial junctures at which the theologian may stop and consider carefully the significance of Levinas' ethical reassessment of alterity in philosophical thought. This is evidenced by Marion's own reliance upon this aspect of Levinas (although it must be said that he departs from Levinas elsewhere). For Marion, theologians also learn from phenomenology the necessity to discover in its objects of study their own substance and meaning, rather than what the world might impose upon them. The bracketing out of the world allows texts to speak according to their own substantive meaning. This requires a hermeneutic of humility before the texts, and this in turn further elaborates the need for theologians to rediscover their vocation as interpreters of a textual tradition that sits anterior to their own work. In particular, theologians are ultimately interpreters of Scripture, and in this Marion also wishes to move beyond the classical centrality of Being as such. For him, the Word of God ought to speak to the human subject on its own terms, and not as a programmatic expression of Being through religious terms and ideas. This is Marion's question for theologians: how might we allow ourselves to be gripped by an iconic conceptualization of our vocation and better allow the phenomenon of Scripture to determine, 'starting from itself and itself alone, the conditions of its reality'.[45] This question is both a theological and a phenomenological question, and one that relies on an answer that may only be evoked in the activity of exegetical reflection. That is to say, the answer is not itself philosophical, but an ethical meeting of the face-to-face with the otherness of the subject at hand. In turn, such an approach takes up Levinas' argument (considered in this book in Chapter 4) that the holy texts foundational to religion can be treated ethically only by allowing their narratives to be read in the light of their original cultural contexts, and according to their own logic. Levinas calls for an authentic reading of these texts which allows their coherence to be met authentically, avoiding all impositions of contemporary bias. In this way, the theologian meets Scripture in the same ethical significance as Levinas' and Marion's invocation of the face-to-face. The theologian does not meet God *qua* God in the texts, but meets the Scriptures *qua* Scripture, and they in turn substantiate the trace of God.

In this, Levinas calls his readers to orientate themselves carefully towards that which lies beyond Being. In recognizing the de-centring of the subject that occurs through the intervention of the Other, the theologian discovers oneself in the dark room described earlier in this chapter. It is to sit without knowledge of one's own, trembling before a provocation that demands an ethical response. In this way, it is a rather emboldened encounter that is initiated outside of the self, even as it gazes insistently upon the self. To rediscover the vocation of the theologian as an ethical endeavour is not to seek out some new path that has not been trod, but to work humbly before the paradoxical nature of revelation as the provocation to act, even as it causes one to recognize a sincere passivity in one's existentiality. In this movement or reorientation *beyond Being* – towards 'being's other' – one finds oneself at a metaphysical impasse. On the one hand, the well-articulated metaphysics of the Western tradition seems to be treated in a high degree of suspicion and doubt. It is deconstructed by Levinas and shown to privilege what he calls the same rather than the Other. In a theologically informed context, Marion opens a movement beyond Being to rediscover a place for philosophizing about revelation within a Christian framework and, ultimately, to find oneself doing theology. Here, it can be admitted that Levinas' call to reconsider the place of Being owes much to a metaphysical framework seeking an ethical foundation. His enticement of readers towards the authenticity of the face-to-face becomes a foundational element in his thought, even as he denies the illusion of such a concept as a foundation as such. In fact, Levinas expresses cynicism about contemporary philosophy's assumption of the 'end of metaphysics'.[46] He asks whether the end of metaphysics has become an idea made meaningless by so many thinkers' attempt to declare it to be so. No, as this book argues, Levinas does not declare the end of metaphysics anymore than he announces the end of Being. Rather, he investigates the problematic rendering of Being (and consequently metaphysics generally) in Western philosophy and reorientates its practitioners towards an ethical responsibility on behalf of the other person. Indeed, Levinas wishes the human subject to be gripped by a Platonic notion of the Good, insofar as it is the proper possession of the self on behalf of the suffering Other. It bypasses the category of the principle of 'choice', for it is a responsibility existent before all freedom to choose is made present. Evil itself is the denial of this responsibility, which in itself is a choice discovered after the provocation of the good in the face of the Other. And so the reorientation of the theologian is one that discovers the passivity of the subject at hand, and recognizes that one thinks and works within a wider 'inefficacy of human action'; a contemporary context in which the ethical response is to return ourselves to the realization that on the 'reverse side of being' is the originary and crucial 'metaphysical antecedence'.[47]

By the 'reverse side' of Being, Levinas refers his readers to 'being's other', which is not the dismantling of Being as such, but of a reorientation towards the other person. He does not favour a facile ignorance of metaphysics nor a juvenile vandalism of Being. For Levinas, Being must be reconsidered, rethought and re-encountered beyond itself, and concretized in the face of the Other, even as the other person bears an alterity that denies the impermeability of Being. For Marion, this is also a means of moving religious thought beyond illicit constructions of the divine that thwart the notion of God as a free agency diffused beyond Being. This is why Marion takes up the notion of the given, and givenness as excess. The effect of God as gift is that the paradox itself becomes the pre-eminent category, rather than the faint trace of a conceptual limitation being placed upon the divine. Marion argues:

> It is therefore no longer, as in metaphysics, the cause that would remain immanent to its effects (supposing that this proposition could ever really be thought without contradiction), but givenness that remains *immanens, non vero transiens* in the gifts.[48]

For Marion, givenness is a movement of the authentic gift of the Other. It remains immanent within a transcendent activity of self-donation. As such, Marion's idea of the gift is an important means by which one aspect of Levinas' own thought can address thinking-beyond-Being. But for Levinas, we are called to act before we are called to think. And the mode of reflection itself must become an action predicated on the state of demanding passivity before otherness. This is itself a paradox; that of enacting passivity before the movement of self-election derived in the face of the Other. In a sense, the highest expression of this in theological terms is not so much the articulation of theological argumentation and dogmatic content, but the liturgical expression of Christian faith as it is practised in concrete forms. For example, in the simple bending of the knee and bowing of the head in genuflection, the human subject embodies a moment of self-abnegation before its divine Other. For the Western Catholic tradition, this is an action performed before the presence of the consecrated bread and wine, believed to be the body and blood of Christ. To the familiar practitioner, the action warrants little notice and becomes a part of the texture of Christian ritual from one Eucharistic celebration to another. In immediate thought, it carries no ethical content and bears no significance outside of the ordinary. And in this way, its habitual practice hides a pedagogy of theological-ethical importance. In the act of genuflection, one has caused the body a restrictive posture that expresses humility in the presence of one who stands higher than the self. It is an act of thankfulness, because the divine presence sits within the shade of the tabernacle as one who is master of the sanctuary, and whose house the church building is intended to materialize. The Christian disciple who genuflects before entering their seat, whether during a Eucharistic celebration or in a spare weekday moment, has subjugated the self in thankfulness for divine hospitality. He or she has escaped the moodiness and worldliness of that which exists outside the church walls and allowed one moment of severe passivity. It is severe because it is a fully embodied exposure to the gaze of the Other from the altar. It stands accused of sin, and yet promised redemption within the same gaze. And as Marion shows in his exegetical reflection, the iconic form of Christ redoubles its saturating presence upon the receiver, so that the person who has genuflected has cause to go out and love the neighbour as their own self, and to care explicitly for those in need. This is not to say for a moment that genuflection, let alone any other liturgical action, implies holiness. Rather, it conveys the opposite; that the human self itself has no holiness to convey, but must passively seek out the holiness of the Other. The touching of the knee to the floor seeks out the face-to-face with the sacramental presence and restores clarity in one's relationship to the mystery of authentic embodied alterity.

The example of genuflection conveys a discrete moment of ethical responsibility in the gaze of the Other upon the self. And while Levinas would not have accepted the Eucharistic context as an authentic encounter with the Other, it must be said that his account of Being's other does not exclude the possibility either. For the Church, God has taken flesh in the Incarnation of Jesus Christ, and his presence is the enactment of otherness as it seeks out to meet the human subject. In Christ, the human person meets another human being – a son, a teacher, a worker, a leader and a brother of others – and in turn also meets one who is known in the height and transcendence of a singular glory. The messianic arrival of the anointed one is, paradoxically, an encounter with that which is truly human. Moreover, that which is truly human is so perfectly united to divinity that the person of Christ becomes a sacrifice that opens the way both to experience the world more authentically and to anticipate a life of glory in which death holds no sway. The call of Christ is an unnerving paradox of suffering within the world and the promise of such a glory. One may recall the poetic words of John Henry Newman:

> And in the garden secretly,
> and on the cross on high,
> should teach his brethren, and inspire
> to suffer and to die.[49]

As Newman saw clearly, the inspiration to live and die resides in the human face of God, embodied in Jesus Christ. A Christian account of the relationship between an authentic life for others and the life of sacrificial self-service is of course paradoxical. The promise of glory and the blood of the martyrs are, for the Christian imagination, intricately linked as anterior to the further growth of the ecclesia and the development of holiness in all those who would be faithful. And in these terms, one moves beyond Being and all its misguided thematizations to break what Levinas refers to as a self-recurrence that has permeated philosophy throughout the modern era.[50] The relationship between the subtle gesture of a genuflection and the grand narrative of those who shed blood for their faith is of immense importance, for it resides completely in the inspiration of suffering that alights in the face of Christ. In the particularity of that face, one finds the concretization of God in terms familiar to both revelation and the essential character of responsibility that Levinas invokes in the human face. Further to this is the mystery that for the vast majority of Christian disciples, the face of Christ is a plurality of faces rendered in multiple paintings, iconography, statues and engravings; a face sketched in every ethnicity and presented in every cultural *mythos*. Always it remains the same face in terms of its significance for the human condition, even as its artistic forms became entangled in local customs and representations. Such a face comes to be seen reflected in other faces, not by means of an unethical mediation, but as the otherwise to the being of the world, who in participating in the world, loves the world back towards itself.

From a theological perspective, the call of Levinas to acquaint ourselves carefully with the nature of ethical responsibility as it permeates the face of the Other, is, perhaps unexpectedly, a notion that Christian tradition is already acquainted with. Again, it needs to be recalled that the God who comes to mind in Levinas' work is not to be equated naively with the God of Abraham, Isaac and Jacob. Nevertheless, the remarkable insights of *Totality and Infinity* and *Beyond Being* constitute a project that does not contradict the Christian notion of Incarnation in its dogmatic content. A phenomenological disclosure of the significance of the face-to-face can only provoke for theologians the unsettling feeling that further attention ought to be paid to the most central and basic dogmatic formularies of faith, especially as they relate to a God who meets human persons in flesh that may be crucified, and a body that may die.

Chapter 3

'*Would* You Like to Do a Bit of Theology?' Levinas and the *Theological Turn*

In an interview given in 1983, Levinas becomes impatient with his interviewer. Having been asked whether the face of the other person is a mediation of God, Levinas interjects with a return question. 'Hold on a minute', Levinas replies, '[n]ow we're getting into theology . . . To me, the other is the other human being. *Would* you like to do a bit of theology?'[1] For Levinas, this is a contemptible thought because it would reduce the person to a mere conduit of a greater alterity. He would rather speak of the word of God reverberating in the face of the Other, and of the Other as itself the event in which God may be thought. The announcement of the Other is a self-disclosure of ethical inviolability, and Levinas insists that it is given without the 'odor' of the 'numinous' and, by extension, a 'holiness' as such.[2]

For Levinas, the language of alterity is philosophically rigorous and not bound to theological flights of poetic or mystical conjecture. Nor is it a metaphorical language; it is an authentic expression of a divine thought that has no origins outside the alterity that permeates the face of the Other. For Levinas, this is, therefore, an authentic ethics. It is a language open to otherness in such a way that the Other's transcendence is maintained. This openness is repeatedly contrasted with philosophical language concerning otherness that seems to traverse the transcendent nature of the other person and induct them into categories of what Levinas calls the same. For example, Levinas takes up the Genesis narrative of Cain and Abel and uses it as a Scriptural rejection of the ontological description of the other person. According to Levinas, the question put to Cain by God is an ethical question, '[w]here is your brother?', whereas Cain's answer is formulated in an ontological vein: 'Am I my brother's keeper?' Such a response is a denial of Abel's ethical significance and commits Cain to an ontology of the other that reduces and circumvents alterity. In this way, Cain's ontological commitment does violence to the singular witness of his brother's needfulness in the world, thus constituting an ontological violence that precedes the fratricide to come. Furthermore, Cain denies the ethical content of the face of his brother and redoubles this contention upon God Himself, introducing into the reduction of the other a troubling diminishment of the ethical perfection of the divine name. That is to say, God's name has become infected with the same ethical content that Cain introduces into human inter-subjectivity. At this point, it is worth recalling that for Levinas, the distinction between revealed theology and natural theology is strong, although his own biblical references render the distinction unstable.

The example of Cain and Abel is one that makes this point very clearly, in which Levinas draws upon a theological narrative to inform and defend his philosophical argument. Such an example is highlighted because it is not unusual in the Levinasian corpus, which in turn explains the vexed position in which some theologians and philosophers find themselves when confronted with Levinas. Such a challenge in interpreting Levinas relates profoundly to a contemporary dispute within philosophy concerning the 'theological turn' in phenomenology, especially among French thinkers. The term itself is intended to be derisive, and originates in a critical work by Dominique Janicaud, who argues that philosophers like Emmanuel Levinas, Jean-Luc Marion, Michel Henry and Jean-Louis Chrétien (but not limited to these four) have departed from the rigorous science of Edmund Husserl's original phenomenological method.[3] By referring to the phenomenological method as a rigorous science, it is helpful to remember the nature of Husserl's hopes for phenomenology. In an essay titled 'Philosophy as Rigorous Science', Husserl develops the notion that despite the grand claim of philosophy as a lofty enterprise reaching towards 'pure' and 'absolute' knowledge, its character as a 'rigorous science' had barely begun in the early to mid-twentieth century.[4] From the fragmented display of previous texts and arguments across millennia of philosophy, Husserl wishes to draw out a more pure philosophy – a phenomenology – that might robustly formulate a theory of essence capable of founding a 'philosophy of the spirit'.[5] Husserl sees in the life of the mind a new phenomenological emergence of exact language that has the capacity to reflect experience within the world. His reference to the spirit is intended to manifest the whole of what it is to experience the world as a human person, without reduction of any part thereof. As Husserl developed his method, he came to defend a strict and logical correlation between the two poles experienced in the experience of any objective data within the world, that of the subject pole of the ego and the world-pole.

For Husserl, phenomenology is a rigorous science in that it recognizes profoundly that each philosopher operates within multiple spheres of 'direct intuition'.[6] As each directly intuits an object/s of philosophical investigation, he or she comes to regard a correlation between the egotistically experienced perspective of the subject pole and the exteriorly directed world-pole, the latter of which remains other to the self. Such a discovery is made because of the *epoché*, in which the self brackets out the world to allow the unique disclosure of the object at hand. In this, Husserl outlines a science that ensures the foundational nature of philosophy to all other sciences, and one in which the true nature of things might be met and received by the philosopher according to their own existential quality and content.

In Levinas and others, this strict or 'rigorous' science is taken to include that which for many Husserlians lies outside the orbit of what was intended by the father of phenomenology. In extending the phenomenological project to consider themes that might be considered religious (such as God), Janicaud claims that such thinkers have turned to theology rather than to phenomenology. Levinas is considered a significant protagonist of the turn because of his metaphysical investment in the Other. This chapter will briefly sketch the contours of phenomenology for readers unfamiliar with its history and basic premises. For those well versed in phenomenology and the contemporary debate concerning the theological turn, this will seem all too simplistic, and a humble request for their patience is offered. For those whose work in theology has not brought them to this debate until more recently, this can offer a beginning and it is hoped they will delve further into an important, and largely unresolved, dispute. Having sketched such contours, this chapter will then seek to show that the concerns raised by Levinas, and in relation to him the work of Marion, carry forth a provocation in a way conducive to a theological ethic of alterity. It will be argued that this helps to indicate a movement towards a theology of embodied alterity, while not losing sight of some of the problems within Levinas' thought identified throughout this book.

Since Edmund Husserl's inception of the phenomenological method in Germany in the late nineteenth and early twentieth centuries, it has grown as a method and as an intellectual movement. Phenomenology is predicated on the basis that things might be 'known in themselves' and that the objective content of any particular phenomena may be described in the manner of its experience. The oft-quoted mantra is, therefore, Husserl's cry, 'back to the things themselves'.[7] Strict phenomenologists have, therefore, been wary of the possibility of metaphysics as it relates to religious experience and the realm of theology was viewed as relying on too many non-phenomenal presuppositions. Since Husserl, certain thinkers, particularly in the French academy, have used the phenomenological method to describe the realm of the affective, and have dealt with themes such as love, death and God. Of these, Emmanuel Levinas and Jean-Luc Marion are notable in their observance of phenomena that seem to cross the distance from philosophy to religion, or alternatively from natural theology to revealed theology. While this is explicit in Marion who revels in such a crossing of the distance, it remains ambiguous in Levinas. For both, phenomena may be described not simply in terms of their observable content, but by the manner in which they are experienced. For example, love is hardly an object to be discovered through the strict observance of Husserl's subject-world distinction, but must be explained in terms of its experiential qualities also; and so affectivity must play a crucial part in phenomenological language if there is any merit in phenomenology at all. This tendency has been criticized robustly as the 'theological turn' in phenomenology. The phenomenological method, especially as it has been modified by Levinas and that of Marion, provides a language with which to situate the development of a Christian ethics that allows itself to be informed by the concrete significance of alterity. Indeed, it situates those of faith to receive the import of otherness not only as a phenomenality within the world, but also as a transcendent movement not reliant on the world as such.

For both Marion and Levinas, there are, in the world, experiences that cannot be reduced to a limited set of explanatory categories. For example, the human person is a surplus of experience that resists facile explanations or ideological description. To speak phenomenologically of the human person, there remains always a surplus of meaning attached to both the subjective experience of what it is to be human and what it is to experience the event of the other person within one's own life-experience. Crude biological, philosophical or economic formulations will not do. This surplus is often referred to as an excess (Marion's 'saturated phenomena') because it appears in such a way that, in effect, fosters a need to seek out a fruitful, exacting language to convey the mystery of human existence. One could only ever speak too little of the dignity and beauty of what appears in the person of another (one might also refer to Levinas' 'infinity' of the Other). An ethical inversion of this statement might also be stated; that we cannot speak too greatly of the value of that which appears before us in the human person. This approach helps to craft an awareness of the phenomena of human personhood in terms of a surplus of dignity and otherness.

Various ethical approaches have been inspired by aspects of the phenomenological method. Its broad remit is such that it remains limited only to what is formally observed, which has provided the basis for areas of enquiry as diverse as Hannah Arendt's understanding of conscience, human dignity and democracy and the ethical system of Max Scheler.[8] The development of phenomenology offers a myriad of such possibilities. Dermot Moran, in his *Introduction to Phenomenology*, makes the following observation:

> . . . phenomenology cannot be understood simply as a
> method, a project, a set of tasks; in its historical form
> it is primarily a set of people, not just Husserl and his
> personal assistants, Edith Stein, Martin Heidegger, Eugen
> Fink, Ludwig Landgrebe, but more broadly his students,
> Roman Ingarden, Hedwig Congrad-Martius, Marvin
> Farber, Dorion Cairns, Alfred Schütz, Aron Gurwitsch,
> and many others, including Max Scheler and Karl
> Jaspers, who developed phenomenological insights in
> contact and in parallel with the work of Husserl. Thus
> phenomenology as a historical movement is exemplified
> by a range of extraordinary diverse thinkers.[9]

Now, this means that phenomenology as a philosophical movement is inimically tied to those who have tested and developed it across its historical development. With Levinas, phenomenology was introduced in France chiefly as the work of Husserl and Heidegger. Its significance cannot be overstated. Simone de Beauvoir gives a memorable account of Jean-Paul Sartre's first encounter with the philosophy of Emmanuel Levinas, which largely began as an introduction to Husserl's phenomenology in the French academy.[10] Sartre was sharing a day out in Paris in 1932, drinking apricot cocktails with Raymond Aron, one of Husserl's students. Stories of the impact phenomenology was having in Germany were filling the air and Sartre was intrigued by this new movement. He sought information from Aron who, delighted by this interest, said to Sartre: 'You see, my little comrade, if you are a phenomenologist, you can talk about this cocktail, and that is philosophy'.[11] According to Beauvoir, Sartre went pale with excitement and rushed to make his first purchase in phenomenology. As charming and probably as mythical as aspects of this story may be, it illustrates something important about phenomenology, and that is that its remit is as broad as the plurality of phenomena. In thinking about Levinas in particular, it is suggested here that his critical engagement with the inter-subjective moment between human persons, and precisely in the manner of their appearing to the self as the Other, constitutes a fruitful means of conceiving of all phenomena. As interesting and sweet to the palate as an apricot cocktail may be, there remains in the visage of the one who lifts it in the Parisian sun, an excessive signification that both speaks of the transcendent, and turns the ethical gaze towards the mystery of the incarnate person. No less than the apricot cocktail, the human person does indeed catch the ethical gaze, and it is shown in what follows how using phenomenological sources such as Emmanuel Levinas provides a grammar of excess by which the person may better be described.

In his work, *Cartesian Meditations: An Introduction to Phenomenology* (first published in French in 1931), Edmund Husserl sought to provide a philosophical system that could provide a universal basis for all other sciences.[12] It is interesting that the book did not make its appearance in German until long after Husserl's death in 1938. Furthermore, its first appearance was in a French translation by Levinas, which alone secures his place in European philosophical history. Levinas could see the radical transformation of philosophy that Husserl had begun substantially before peers such as Sartre and Merleau-Ponty. Indeed, phenomenology, as represented in the *Meditations*, came to be seen by Husserl as itself a universal science, whatever his students and intellectual heirs thought. In his dialogue with the thought of René Descartes, Husserl's attempt at a universal framework in which the philosophical sciences could share a common system was understood as a transcendental phenomenology. Here, he outlines some of the key aspects of this new philosophy, which is predicated on knowing phenomena in themselves. Phenomenology, for Husserl, was the process by which we would understand the object of intention through an experiential intuition. Intentionality describes the subjective aim of the ego towards the object that gives rise to a correlation between the subject and the object, which in turn is manifest as a concrete experience within the life of the subject. Husserl saw his work as a radical departure from the limitations of the Cartesian system, but one that still owes much to Descartes. The Cartesian idea of the infinite as it exists within the human mind is a crucial point of connection between Husserl and Descartes, although for Husserl it initiates a process of surplus within all of existence. As discussed above, an important feature of Husserl's strict phenomenological system is the *epoché*, a strategy the philosopher undertakes that seeks to bracket out the world. In this way, one may receive more clearly the datum of a particular object of intentionality.[13] In bracketing out or suspending the world, the philosopher (or as Husserl puts it, the philosophizing philosopher) frees the particular object within the intentional life of the ego. It could be said that in such a movement, the philosopher is freed from the natural attitude about the world, and that the world is present as a spatiotemporal horizon unconstituted by the life of the subject.

For example, rather than looking upon the green tree frog as a manifestation of a species half hidden in the undergrowth of a vibrant ecosystem, one focuses on the presence of a *particular* frog, staring into its pupils and recalling the significance of one creature in all its singularity. Of course, the frog does not constitute or represent the world. In being captivated by the beauty of the frog in its otherness and singularity, one does not at the same time reject or annihilate the world in which both the frog and the self are inescapably situated. The horizon of the world remains constant. One does not reject the world, or disregard it. Rather, one strips one's perception of the world back from one's intentional gaze and humbly seeks to allow the object at hand to speak in its own terms. The otherness of the frog is to be attended to within the parameters of its own unique givenness. There is an ethics to such a bracketing out, in that it searches out the truth of a thing according to its own measure, and without interring in one's reading of its significance any other imposition or counter-claim. It is, therefore, a posture of humility.

Ethics is of central concern to the phenomenological project of Emmanuel Levinas. Indeed, Levinas, against the ontology of Martin Heidegger, proposes ethics as 'first philosophy', and develops a phenomenological understanding of the Other in which the self is always responsible for the good of the Other. Levinas considers the phenomenon of the face, in which the other person is borne to one's consciousness and evokes a response of utter and complete responsibility. In *Totality and Infinity*, Levinas devotes the second and third sections of the book to his consideration of the face. In Section III, he considers the nature of the appearing of the face to one's senses as an '*epiphany*' in consciousness.[14] He specifically considers the relationship between ethics and the face, by which he seeks to show in the appearance of the face a concrete social presence that evades all of one's own ability to wield power.[15] In fact, even at the point where the self might seek to contort the face and to restrict it in some way, it proves resistant. Levinas does not naively mean that the human face has a physical strength that resists all provocation. Rather, he means that the power of the face to bear witness to the otherness of the person in itself cannot be superseded. There is an infinity of meaning here, in which the trace of the transcendence borne of the face comes to mind and receives its intuitive presence. Power can, therefore, no longer take from the face its ethical content or, to put it another way, the face effaces all possibility of its alterity being robbed or reduced. One person may murder another, and yet, even then, the act of murder may never obliterate the alterity that alights upon the human visage. Even in that moment, the presence of the face haunts the mind of the murderer, and clings on in the social memory in a trace that insists on a search for justice. The wider community's search for justice also reveals a trace of the infinity of the face. The moment of murder, for Levinas, is never an actualization of power, but its very renouncing.[16] As the murderer takes life from a victim, the victim becomes the lingering judge whose alterity is never diminished in the experience of the world. Levinas recognizes the presence of power, but only in the sense that murder desires power over another, and instead finds itself opposed by the presence of the Other, in whom there is an infinite overcoming of the very power of power.[17]

Levinas takes a further turn here, in that he locates the real power of the face as found in its 'unforeseeableness'; in its reaction to the event of conflict.[18] That is to say, in confronting the murderer, the face may fall to the violence of sheer will and physicality, but the trace of possibility is always an infinity of possible outcomes; the face is unpredictable. Even under a legal burden of duress or in the event of torture, the face bears an ethical power over its own dignity that cannot be foreseen. To quote Levinas:

> This infinity, stronger than murder, already resists us in his face, is his face, is the primordial *expression*, is the first word: "you shall not commit murder." The infinite

paralyses power by its infinite resistance to murder,
which, firm and insurmountable, gleams in the face of
the Other, in the total nudity of his defenceless eyes, in
the nudity of the absolute openness of the Transcendent.
There is here a relation not with a very great resistance,
but with something absolutely *other*: the resistance of
what has no resistance – the ethical resistance.[19]

Levinas means more than the face, but locates in it a unique
witness to the perfect otherness of every other person whom
the self encounters. Levinas constructs his account of the
face with this initial description that seems to co-align with
incarnate presence. This might indicate that incarnate presence
signifies the physical and spatial continuum in which two or
more bodies may be met. Nevertheless, Levinas does not mean
less than the human face in its bare nudity or typical experience,
and nor is he giving a clear account of incarnate existence in
itself. In other words, Levinas does not mean the quiddity of
the face as it is perceived in our friend or lover, or indeed the
faces of those we meet in the street or in the busy commute.
He affirms those faces, but seeks to inculcate an appreciation
for the category of the face as it exists beyond and transcendent
to the face in its appearance. The face is, paradoxically, the
alterity of the other person in the event of its appearing. One
might think of those whose ethical demands come urgently,
even if they have not been met in typical sociality: the cries
of the poor on television, the newspaper accounts of children
slain in a far-away war and the unborn whose only trace lies in
secret memories and statistics on a medical record. These faces
have not been met and touched by the human eye or hand,
nor can they speak in conversation. They are not en-fleshed in
the world that one inhabits in the way a spouse or a friend is
incarnated in the daily routine. Yet they remain insistent in an
ethical demand that one responds well. For each of them, a face
demands an ethical response. The infinity of the face reveals
not only the ethical demand it makes of the self for it, but also

the perfect distance between one's own will and the Other, in which an infinity of the face is made immanent in human sociality. Levinas provides a phenomenological description of the face, but always with his concern for what he deems the fundamentally ethical demand of the face of the Other; that which signifies alterity.

In the fourth and last section of *Totality and Infinity*, entitled 'Beyond the Face', Levinas outlines his notion of the transcendent character of the face in its inter-subjectivity, which moves further beyond mere temporality. Consciousness and time are predicated on the welcoming of alterity, by which the Other is known to the self as one that can never truly be known.[20] Even in this unknowability, there is in Levinas a subjective turn to the presence of another who may at least be met and recognized, even if a true knowledge is evasive. Levinas describes the infinite trace: 'To be infinitely – infinition – means to exist without limits, and thus in the form of an origin, a commencement, that is, again, as an existent'.[21] The face reveals not simply an alterity that is overbearing, but also an incarnate existence in which the singular selfhood of the Other is made present and available to care for responsibly. The ethical call is indeed universal, but also localized in a strict focus upon human existentiality.

A significance to the category of the face is particularly pronounced in the work of Jean-Luc Marion, much of whose work has developed a phenomenology of the gift. His work is explored in some detail in Chapter 2, but here also his notion of the saturated phenomenon is of interest. Marion's consideration of the gift has led him to view some forms of objective intuition as experiences of excess. He speaks of events that seem to flood one's intuition, exceeding what one may think, say or discern in the event. Certainly, Marion insists that particular objective intuitions of that which lay outside the self may be interpreted as limited and categorical. For example, a table does not appear to have an excess of meaning that goes beyond the limits of what might be formally described. The table is coloured brown and made of timber. It is evenly shaped and stands against the wall, and so forth. However, Marion views certain other experiences as excessive in their signification. A table is also the scene of an important meal, or the reception of sad news. In his account of *eros*, Marion locates an incarnate inter-subjectivity that also has the capacity to saturate one's interpretative reception of objects of intentionality. Marion notes the dearth of rich philosophical interest into the meaning or nature of love. Philosophers have generally failed to give a full and nuanced account of the phenomenon of love, avoiding all of its social and ethical implications in a bid for metaphysical truth displayed in purely cognitive categories. Marion argues in *The Erotic Phenomenon*:

> Philosophy today no longer says anything about love,
> or at best very little. And this silence is for the better,
> because when philosophy does venture to speak of love
> it mistreats it or betrays it . . . and for good reason, for
> they know, better than anyone, that we no longer have
> the words to speak of it, nor the concepts to think about
> it, nor the strength to celebrate it.[22]

Marion speaks of an experience for which contemporary culture has lost the words to describe. In this aporia, he locates a space in which phenomenology might discover a certain *richesse* that pervades human experience. As such, Marion attempts a description of the phenomenon of love. He does so informed by his previous work on the saturated phenomenon and its basis in the transcendent movements of the giving, and receiving of the gift. As a phenomenological 'source', Marion is of course criticized by Janicaud for utilizing the notion of saturated phenomena to 'smuggle' in theological concepts.[23] For Janicaud, phenomenology ought to accept the modern dethroning of philosophy from atop the other sciences, to avoid what he terms a 'contemporary overestimation of its capacities'.[24] Marion takes an opposing tact in that he finds in phenomenology an essential openness to human experience that does not bracket out God as such.

Furthermore, Marion speaks of the thought of 'God without Being', of the rising of God without anchoring it in the metaphysical framework of Being as such.[25] This achieves the possibility of philosophy opening itself fundamentally to a study of God, but within what Robyn Horner calls a 'conditional legitimacy' for ontology.[26] That is to say, Marion overcomes metaphysics through an approach to theology that relies on a limited attainment of the object at hand, and of a humble acceptance that an object can only be recognized rather than cognized and received rather than appropriated. Horner highlights this in reference to the possible critique that Marion's account relies too strongly on the act of faith, which in turn carries at least the indicative possibility of a dogmatic commitment. But Marion, in describing the saturated phenomena as breaking all limiting horizons of intuition, defends his theological reflections in the context of doing phenomenology. Chiefly, he views the exclusion of all transcendence by the phenomenological reduction – the 'bracketing out' of the world – as itself an overextension of phenomenology and an absurd limitation of the philosophical task. In so doing, he asserts the very real existential moment of saturation, one that is recognized as existing beyond concepts and objective categories and certainly beyond the possibility of perfect description. The theological trajectory is always present in Marion's work, which accounts for his argument that God-as-charity is an iconic moment of saturation which upsets other categories. For Marion, the face of the Other must be, in Levinas' terms, distinguished from the other person, even as Marion holds to the particular alterity of the Other. Here, love interrupts as God, for the transcendence of the divine is a directionality beyond and not contained within being in the world. There is a startling self-assertion in the act of love, even as it gives itself over for the Other. Marion writes:

> For love requires the personalization of the face, for two reasons; first because I can only love in an oath, where just such an other will say to me alone, uniquely and in the first person, "Here I am!"; next, because I can only love if my flesh is eroticized to give to the other her or his own flesh, but with a finite eroticization, limited to a single other in a given time – I can give only one flesh, and thus I can only give it in particular.[27]

In other words, love seeks out and desires the good of the person represented in the face. Even in the context of erotic love, the giving over of flesh from one person to another becomes an exemplary form of an ethical response to the other person. One of the prime examples Marion uses for a saturated phenomenon is in an essay in which he builds directly on Levinas' idea of the face and finds a moment of saturation as well as an ethical demand. More can be said of Marion's development of these themes. In his book, *In Excess, Studies of Saturated Phenomena*, Marion completes the third part of his trilogy on phenomenology, following the books, *Reduction and Givenness* and *Being Given*.[28] In that final instalment, he deploys four concrete examples of phenomena that, in their givenness, are received to the point of saturation in one's consciousness. They are outlined under the headings, 'The Idol or the Radiance of the Painting', 'Flesh or the Givenness of the Self', 'The Icon or the Endless Hermeneutic' and 'In the Name: How to Avoid Speaking of It'.

These owe a significant debt to Levinas' infinity of the Other, as reflected in the face of the Other. In each of them, otherness draws near and opens up a way to look both beyond Being and, indeed, beyond philosophy as it is traditionally conceived. In utilizing both Marion and Levinas, one can retrieve an idea of the transcendent nature of the human person in such a way that it resists any form of ethical reduction.

One way of describing such a phenomenon is to suggest that the *telos* of the Other does not find its expression in the self. The self must entirely reject any notion that a person finds its end within one's personal sphere of thought and action. Indeed, the *telos* of any other person also acts as an anthropological surplus, of an infinite directionality not limited to the self as it undergoes its own life-experience in the ordinary world. Such a *telos* always exceeds the correlation between the life of the *ego* and the object constituted within the *ego*. We may begin, phenomenologically speaking, by suggesting that the event of an other in one's field of social purview is borne in one's own mind. The presence of the other person interrupts one's own thoughts and causes the self to begin again in one's recollections and understanding. Even the most familiar of persons will enter the field of one's consciousness with a newness, in that he or she begins something anew under one's gaze (or within one's earshot, or mediated through other sense and informational data). In the event of the other's appearing, one's own apprehension is disturbed and opened up to that which is other to the oneself.

Familiar faces interrupt one's self-subsisting egoism, impacting on the self as if it were a novel event in each singular appearance. Yet, even here, the other person's entrance into one's field of view is not limited to an immediate presence. There is a *telos* which only the other person may encapsulate, but whose trajectory cannot be contained or quantified. The limiting factor of this *telos*, as it appears, is the epistemological boundary that may begin as an ethical origin within the self. Levinas of course states that time itself is of and for the other, and that the other person originates in a time before time, asserting an ethical consequence that goes beyond mere temporality. Yet to take a step back from this reflection, even assuming it is true, is to recognize that the self does not share the originary moment with the Other. The alterity of the other always precedes every I. The other's presence first interrupts one's consciousness as a new beginning, one that assigns the self as the elect who must act responsibly for the other. Levinas insists upon the pre-reflexive call of responsibility, which is issued in the space of another's alterity. One cannot collude others in one's personal interest or agenda, nor may one categorize the other person under the subjugation of a name that he or she does not recognize. The other's face is transcendent to the self. Rather, the person of the self (which is always in the concreteness of the flesh) is at the other's disposal and answers an ethical call by offering everything for the sake of the other. In the face, this ethical demand is made manifest, with all the force of a mysterious sociality that cannot be fathomed or explained. The other appears as a mystery and marks out the vocation of the self. The oneself stands accused and elected for a particular task.

While the *telos* of the Other is also mystery, one's own *telos* is revealed as *ethos*: the end of the self is to be found in the responsible living out for the beginning of an Other. Once again, Levinas situates a calling of the self towards its vocation within the overbearing context of an alterity that cannot be contained. Even in the tamest, most vulnerable passivity of the suffering Other, an inherent wildness plays its part. It is a hidden wildness, shying away from sensory awareness, yet it is present in an ethical content that is demanding and unpredictable or, in another word, infinite.

In a world of persons in which the notion of personhood is at stake – be it the human embryo which has no en-fleshed voice, or the stateless refugee facing a foreign regime without due process – ethical enquiries are enhanced by the insights of Levinas. In responding to the face, one discovers that one does not have the simplicity of a choice, as if ethics could be watered down to mitigated options upon a page of plural opportunities. One is bereft of choice and assigned a vocation before the Other. Such a vocation places the Christian notion of discipleship within the phenomenological reach of contemporary thought.

For example, in Matt 4:18-20, the briefest of narratives explains how the first apostles were chosen by Jesus. While walking along the shoreline, Jesus witnesses in Galilee two brothers, Simon (Peter) and his brother Andrew. They are going about their habitual work without doing harm to others, as far as the reader can be aware. Yet they are issued a demand from a voice that asserts authority without violence or intrigue: 'Follow me, and I will make you fishers of men'. The vocation they are called to does not deny what they already were – fishermen – but raises it to the level of divine service. They would continue to cast a net of a different kind. The skills and training of each man was not, as it happens, put aside, as if the gifts of the world were discarded completely. Rather, these fishermen brought these gifts to enact a service to God and the world with an urgency that can only be understood by virtue of the one who issued the call. For example, as fishermen, they would have followed the tides and the cycle of the moon, fully aware at all times as to how winds and currents might affect the quality of their catch. They would probably have had habits of early morning duties and a routine of multiple responsibilities. Such skills would be translated into the context of human inter-subjectivity, in which they would proclaim to others a message that did not originate in them, but would be mediated through them. In Simon was to be crafted a Petrine ministry to provide stability and concord to the Christian faithful. In Andrew was to be found the icon of the true disciple, and he would become a patron for the Church in East and in West. For both, a cross would seal their death in the memory of martyrs. Here is one example in which the place of vocation is made by virtue of a specific, particular call.

For both brothers, the call of Christ would result in suffering and death. The phenomenological discovery of the nature of the ethical call in itself holds together the transcendent nature of the election by the other with the requirement that one suffer and self-abnegate. This is relevant in the contemporary moment, in which the theological importance placed upon vocation might be heard as incoherent nonsense. Levinas retrieves the placing of the vocational call as itself indicative of an election that originates in alterity, and by virtue of otherness bears the mark of authority. It strips bare the self and contends with the self's conflicting desires to serve only the self at the detriment of the other person. It is an election that denies the sovereignty of self-autonomy. And this election, therefore, serves the person *as* person; as a uniquely irreducible gift that obligates the self on the behalf of the other. What Simon and Andrew understood in the moment of election is recognized philosophically by Levinas. Yet, what Simon and Andrew experienced was an explicitly theological moment, in which God transgresses the boundary between the profane and the holy. God does not simply speak to the two from an alterity characterized chiefly by its transcendence, but from an alterity that stirs up the sand as it plods across the shoreline. Such an alterity – an *embodied* alterity – requires both the austere responsibility that Levinas describes and the recognition that revealed theology attends to both the phenomenality of inter-subjectivity as it is experienced *and* God's self-disclosure in the world. At times, such a relationship between theology and phenomenology will be a tension, but such a tension is fruitful.

Now, envisaging a fruitful, albeit tense relationship between theology and phenomenology is to engage positively with the narrative of the history of phenomenology. Indeed, the story of phenomenology has, and could be said, to be the story of twentieth-century European philosophy.[29] Husserl might be its father in a formal intellectual and spiritual sense, but its origins can be ploughed in the divergences of Western philosophy for many centuries before. Levinas, for example, relies firmly on Descartes' discovery of the infinite within the *cogito* as confirmation of the idea of God, within the strictures of modern philosophy.

As a mode of philosophical enquiry, phenomenology has served the political projects of thinkers as diverse as Martin Heidegger in *Being and Time* (Heidegger himself notoriously advocated policies of German National Socialism, causing a significant rift with Levinas and others), Jean-Paul Sartre, notably *Being and Nothingness* (his phenomenologically inspired existentialism bore a complex relationship with his commitment to Marxism), not to mention figures such as Edith Stein, the Jewish-Christian convert whose mysticism was enlivened by Husserl's new philosophy and whose humanism in the face of totalitarianism continues to inspire others. There is no obvious ethical or political route to follow when one employs phenomenology as one's mode of intellectual operation. Yet, a significantly high proportion of phenomenologists have engaged actively with politics of one kind or another. But politics always gives form to an *ethos*. At the very least, we might make the observation that a philosophy centred upon the manner in which one experiences a thing 'in itself' appears to draw some into an engagement with politics. Phenomenology, in opening up the world to a rich discovery by those who would persevere in its essential methodology, seems to open up possibilities also for acting within the world, which in turn leads to politics. After all, in bracketing out the world, one is attempting an act of humility by purging one's investigations of their presuppositions before the object of investigation. Such a humility requires a sense of the ethical responsibility one has as a philosopher, both before the object in question and before others in the world.

Whether or not Husserl's gesture of the phenomenological *epoché* is even possible (and many have said that it is not), it seems to open up the possibility for a bracketing out of the interests of the world in which an ethical gaze is directed. That is to say, phenomenology insists upon an attempt to remove ourselves from false interest and a personal investment in the object of our gaze which might, in turn, actually reduce the object to our own personal needs, interests and indulgences. If the object of investigation is the human person, the bracketing out of the world is a crucial factor in recognizing the person as a unique other to oneself, and allows one to receive the other, not as a crude collective of categories one can mark off a list (e.g. rationality, physicality, imagination, a heartbeat), but as a transcendent personal value which exceeds all one's ways of knowing. The other person is a surplus of significance. There is, if ethics is done in such a way, a requirement that the other is received as an infinity of meaning, one which saturates the gaze and issues to the self a responsibility that is utterly demanding.

Now, Levinas' approach has always held a tense relationship with phenomenology broadly speaking. While he owes much to the basic structure of phenomenological methodology, the 'theological turn' identified by Janicaud highlights the problem of whether Levinas' work is still within the intellectual tradition of phenomenological inquiry as such. Levinas' discovery of the reversal of the two poles – the giver and the receiver – and the inversion of intentionality this relies upon marks him as offering a unique development of the phenomenological method. While Janicaud claims that this places Levinas outside of phenomenology as Husserl defined it, it must be acknowledged that the philosophical context phenomenologists work within is better explained as an intellectual style or approach that presumes a high degree of flexibility. It is inflected in various ways with no certain boundaries and, as Levinas shows, no phenomenological orthodoxy exists to modify the work of its practitioners. In any case, Levinas' discovery of the reverse intentionality in which one is looked upon and accused by the Other cannot be thought without the initial phenomenological reduction. In this way, Levinas cannot be read apart from phenomenology.

In terms of the tension that exists between phenomenology and Levinas' unique approach, a theologian would be appropriately hesitant in binding a theological perspective strongly to a particular phenomenological strand. For instance, the various tropes in Levinas which appeal so directly to theological language – the Other, God, transcendence and so forth – do not operate in isolation from the phenomenological context in which Levinas writes. It would, therefore, be a cloddish endeavour to extract those terms without their phenomenological reference, and furthermore it would simply be dishonest to insert them uncritically into a theological topography. This is not to assume a sharp distinction between theology and phenomenology, but it does grant a healthy respect for the bounds in which thinkers have worked across the tradition in both theology and philosophy more broadly. The phenomenological achievements of Levinas are such that they do not deny the theologian an entry point in considering alterity as an event that elects its own particular authority over the self, and in fact open a way through which philosophy and theology might communicate on an honest and dialogical platform.

One might call to mind the witness of St Paul in the Areopagus, in which the apostle to the Gentiles preaches a revelation of the unknown God (Acts 17:22-34). This is an important example from the inchoate Church that shows explicit contact between Christianity and Greek philosophical and cultural forms of thought. Paul stood before the 'men of Athens' and drew their attention to the famed altar to the unknown God. In a remarkable display of missional nuance and cultural understanding, Paul explains the resurrection of the Messiah as the fulfilment and revelation of the God of which the altar called to mind. Following his exposition, Paul receives some who came to believe, and from others suffers the mockery of jeers and rejection. In this Athenian context of public debate, Paul embodies an image from which philosophical theologians may take heart. Paul does not relinquish the Gospel granted to him as a gift (as if that was in his remit), but rather announces it in the symbolic language of a context that is both liturgical and intellectually demanding.

The Areopagus was a place both of sacral worship and public debate. In this way, Paul stepped into a tension that exists between the act of faith and the demands of reasoned thought. He enacted in that tension a form of engagement that both respected his interlocutors and issued a demanding apologetic for them to raise their minds and hearts to a radically new concept, in which incarnation and resurrection are pivotal points of divine disclosure. But there is something more, in that Paul does not enter upon the context of the Athenian Rock of Ares without invitation. The narrative (according to Acts 22:15) tells of Paul's arrival in Athens, which faces him as a city of idols. Paul's spirit is 'provoked' (Acts 22:16) and so he enters the Synagogue and the marketplace to reason. On catching the attention of some (especially the Epicurean and Stoic philosophers), Paul is *invited* to the Areopagus. In fact, the text indicates a rather more brisk movement from the marketplace towards the Areopagus, which for the Athenians held the place of divine legal authority. It was a court as well as a place of debate. The significance of Paul's invitation cannot be overstated. His was not a mission to the Athenians that interrupted their religious and cultural habits with bravado and contempt. Rather, he first reasons with them and then, on the basis of his claims concerning Jesus and the resurrection (Acts 22:18), he is summoned onwards to articulate his case further.

The tension between the Synagogue and Marketplace with the Areopagus is not traversed, but informed by the witness to the *Logos* in both. The Pauline proclamation is to follow the provocation of the spirit 'within him' (Acts 22:16) and to reason without compromise to those who would hear. The Christological foundation upon which Paul's case is built is also the bridge between the Synagogue/Marketplace and the Areopagus, and so the tension becomes itself a moment of reasonable grace, making possible a dialogue between Christian theology and Greek philosophy.

To translate this important relationship of creative Christologically informed tension to the discussion of Levinas, it is important to grasp the point that Levinas makes no claim to do theology. His is a critical stance in relation to theology. Levinas refers to 'theology' with a suspicious disposition, at one point saying that 'theological language destroys the religious situation of transcendence'.[30] For

Levinas, the very idea that what is signified (*signifié*) might be limited in meaning to the signifier (*signifiant*) is an ethical mistake common to theology. In other words, the God who is signified in the theological description that signifies, cannot, by definition, be a transcendent God. Levinas argues that theology is an example of the mistaken notion that God, as the object of science, might be contained within a subjective discourse contained within reason. Reason would be simply a violent rendition of interpreting what is other as the same. Levinas is concerned at any ontic tendency that circumscribes God into Being, as has been described in other chapters here. Levinas prefers to mark out a subtle means of confessing an ethical theology, or alternatively, by approaching the work of theology such that it might become what Michael Purcell calls, 'ethically redeemed'.[31] It does so by attending responsibly to the neighbour or the Other. This is why Levinas makes a distinction between revealed theology and what he calls 'natural theology', which is a necessary means of assessing the accent and voice of God in Scripture, and to discern better the transcendence that arises in the face of the other person.[32] Such a distinction allows for the space Levinas indicates to theologians to reassess their work and imagine a *theo*-logic as a science of the ethical, and not only as a reasoned defence for faith. By 'revealed theology', Levinas indicates the explicitly Christian work of those who seek to think and pray within an ecclesial context. Theologians of this variety take seriously the dogmatic content of faith and refer to Scripture in the light of faith as an articulated commitment, without falling into philological tendencies or simplistic historicism. Revealed theology is exemplified by the significant voices of Christian intellectual history; figures such as Irenaeus, Augustine, Thomas Aquinas, Martin Luther, John Calvin, and in more recent times, thinkers such as Karl Barth, Karl Rahner and Hans Urs von Balthasar. On the other hand, 'natural theology' is less easily defined. It includes the work of these thinkers, but is less reliant on Christian doctrines to hang its themes and approaches. It is more a subtle movement or approach that signifies the notion of God as an idea in the realm of discernible phenomenality, and is as likely to be incorporated by a philosopher of religion as by a theologian so named. Levinas is positively inclined towards this type of theology. While he takes up theological language, he is always moving in a direction in which intentional analysis is 'the search for the concrete'.[33] In this directionality, the very idea of God without being arises, at least inasmuch as it belongs to Levinas' thought, and resists a containment of the signified within the signifier. God cannot be limited to a sign, and if he is indeed a Word or *Logos*, it remains an utterance that arrives in excess of itself, breaking the limits of the sign. The Word is surplus to itself.

Such an account does not deny theology its operation, but hints strongly at its own requirement to undergo a redemptive self-evaluation that privileges alterity. It will not do so by turning to a truncated revealed theology in the way that Levinas critiques, but rather as a theology that attends to revelation with as much seriousness as it does to the material circumstances of the world. Theology will turn again to God, but without refraining from a directionality to the poor, the widow and the orphan who confronts human experience in a contemporary moment. That is to say, theology will attend to incarnate existence within the materiality of the world and discover the place in which God is witnessed to by the least of these. For a tradition that values Incarnation as a dogma, it seems strange that it might do otherwise.

Throughout this chapter, a focus has been maintained upon Levinas in the light of the question concerning the 'turn to theology'. Rather than framing this in terms of the argument concerning phenomenological orthodoxy *per se*, it has been described in the light of what is opened up in the impatient and restless question of Levinas in an otherwise calm and reflective interview, '*Would* you like to do a bit of theology?' Levinas expresses more than a little consternation at the question concerning mediation between the Other and God, a notion that he rejects. Levinas wishes to use theological language without recourse to the dogmatic content of religious belief. As has been argued here, this is not the fencing off of a dogmatic faith in itself, but the anxious rebuttal of a theology that seeks to contain 'God' within the conjecture of a rational science. Theology, for Levinas, may have a place in either its 'revealed' or 'natural' guises (although he prefers the latter), but the crucial point is that it must remain attentive to the gleam of the face of the Other. Theology is not privileged to sit apart from the other person, and is called to respond to, and for, the welfare of the other. Because, as we have argued elsewhere, theology is a task, it must be a performative expression of embodied care for the other person, even as it also attends to its own doctrinal heritage.

Indeed, it is further argued in this chapter that theology can achieve nothing fruitful if it does not attend well to its own texts and to its own living tradition. Such a tradition opens itself to the otherness of the other, placing itself first always before the possibility of God without reduction to a rarefied conceptualization. The theologian faces Scripture without falling into philology. And in turning towards the world, the theologian crosses a distance between the Synagogue and marketplace towards the Areopagus without cultural imposition; driven by the spirit, reasoning with the philosophers and ultimately invited by the wise to explain the invisible and the unknown. In this, the theologian has no hegemony over others, but might find in Levinas' 'theological turn' a significant moment in which phenomenology confirms the demand made in the event of alterity. This is the truth that Levinas takes from Husserl and the horrors of the twentieth century: 'The things that we have within our horizon always overflow their content'.[34] Such a surplus, remarkably, is discovered acutely in the rigorous science of Husserlian phenomenology, and theology may learn from this. As such, the theologian may detect in Levinas a turn that liberates the distance between philosophy and the task of theology. This distance – an anxious space between the disciplines – becomes an engaging venture of mutual discovery, liberating theology and calling it to enact more perfectly its vocation before alterity. It is suggested, therefore, that the appropriate answer to Levinas' question, '*Would* you like to do a bit of theology', is in truth, 'in responding to you Monsieur, I already *am*'.

Chapter 4

The Disturbance of Theology

At the beginning of this book, Levinas is described as one who unsettles established foundations. His radical critique of Western philosophy is a disestablishment of its ontological moorings. He rebukes the classical centrality of Being for its disregard of the Other and its debasement of difference. Levinas not only issues his critique with a poetic rendering of alterity, but also re-crafts philosophy such that ethics is the primary category through which one may philosophize. In this way, ethics is 'first philosophy'.[1] For Levinas, the mode of thinking itself is a means of representation in which philosophy acts as an immanent presence. To think is to philosophize and to philosophize is to act. Ethics is first philosophy because the latter is not only a 'knowledge of immanence, it is immanence itself'.[2] This relies on the immediacy of the Other and his or her need. That is to say, the other person interrupts the self-consciousness of the work of the philosopher and cores away at one's subjective response to otherness. This conception of ethics begins not with the self but in that which is absolutely other, and so it is not limited to philosophy but to every act of thought and word in a plurality of difference. Theology is implicated in this reappraisal of the ethical relationship.

Explicitly, Levinas distanced himself from theology. He was concerned at theology's appropriation of the category 'God' into a 'thematization', which circumvents the divine into the thematic structure of Being.[3] In his view, the coincidence of God with Being was an erroneous philosophical move. It restricts the idea of God with an ontological limit instead of recognizing the overwhelming excess of the biblical notion of God. In an essay on 'God and Philosophy', he argues precisely that the *cogito* of Cartesian philosophy cannot carry God in a thought, but experiences God as an interruption.[4] Descartes' 'I' is a finite subject who awakens to itself not in its own strength, but when faced with the infinity of the Other. In fact, the otherness of God breaks up the *cogito* and shows it to be utterly passive. The idea of God arises in this subjective experience of inner disorder and fragmentation, an idea that so exceeds the 'meaning' and 'rationality' of Western philosophy that it can only be named as 'an-archic'.[5] This disorder of the self is brought to light as the idea of God presents itself to the human subject. The infinity of God (what Levinas calls the 'Infinite') is an interrogator and an accuser of the self. It arises in an infinity that refuses the limitations of time – both ancient and new – and stands as a judge of the self and of philosophy. It judges in the sense that the oneself becomes aware of its ethical responsibility in the face of all otherness; of its disquieting passivity over which it has no control and the pressing requirement that it put aside all pretension of worth and wisdom. The thought of God rises in judgement, but also with a calling out of the self in the concern for others in their need and distress.

The otherness of God, for Levinas, brings to light the anarchic fragmentation of the self in the face of each other person. God remains not only other, but also the glory of that which cannot be objectified or categorized in Being; God is 'other than the other', 'other otherwise', even 'transcendent to the point of absence' and so forth.[6] The experience of alterity Levinas describes is ultimately beyond words. He continually revises each new turn of phrase invoked to explain the idea of otherness, seeming to strain at the limits of language to reach the point of understanding. And just as he reaches that point, he insists that understanding is itself not the goal, but rather it is a stage on the way to enacting the disinterested, self-effacing responsibility that alterity demands of each of us.

This is an insistent gnawing away at the self for the sake of the Other. Levinas rebukes theology for thinking God-in-Being and overlooking this crucial aspect of what it is to be faced with the thought of God. It is not the name of God he finds problematic, nor in an authentic thought concerning God. It is rather the thematization of God, whose name cannot be thematized, that Levinas finds troubling. Rather, he says that the first religious discourse begins in the fact of being looked upon by God, of sitting passively before his gaze. The 'here I am' said to the other person (the neighbour), and the responsibility to act on their behalf is given to the self in God's own words.[7] In a way, the 'here I am' issues a demand already, long before specific commands and religious responsibilities are encoded.

Levinas believes the moment of divine command begins in a 'pure ethics' that begins with the other person and the 'here I am'.[8] In the unique face of the Other, the significance of the word *God* comes to mind. Levinas does not spend any length of time analysing particular theologians or theologies to prove his critique. His account of theology's problematic rendering of God-language in a thematization does not rely on specific engagement with theology *per se*, but on theology's close relationship with Western philosophy in historical recollection. This in itself is revealing, for it indicates already that among the various paths of different theologians, and against the backdrop of the twentieth century (rich in theological debate), that other ways of conceiving theology are not considered by Levinas. This shows that theology has a richer, more complex history in its own right than Levinas recognizes.

Theologians have responded to the provocation of Levinas in a number of ways. For example, Robyn Horner outlines three main ways in which Christian theologians have adopted Levinas' thought.[9] Because these three ways are at the forefront of attempts to answer Levinas theologically, the names Horner highlights are worth repeating.

First, Horner describes the way some have sought to bring Levinas into dialogue with significant theologians of the twentieth century. Contemporary work by figures such as Richard J. Beauchesne, Yves Bizeul, M. T. Desouche, David F. Ford, Glenn Morrison, Michael Purcell, Michele Saracino, Steven G. Smith and Graham Ward develops a dialogue between Levinas and what, for theology, constitutes some of the great minds of recent thought. These include Karl Rahner, Hans Urs von Balthasar, Karl Barth, Eberhard Jüngel and Bernard Lonergan. In bringing Levinas into dialogue with these thinkers, there remain various divergences to negotiate, especially in terms of their different treatments of terms like God, let alone their personal faith commitments.

Second, some have tried to rethink various theological themes by integrating perspectives derived from Levinas. Horner lists Marie Baird, Michael Barnes, J. F. Bernier, Roger Burggraeve, David F. Ford, J. F. Lavigne, David J. Livingston, Anselm Kyongsuk Min, Glenn Morrison, F. Poche, Michael Purcell, Michele Saracino, Derek Simonn, J. P. Strandjord, Andrew Tallon, Gabriel Vahanian, Guy Vanderveldem, M. Vannin, Terry A. Veling, Stephen Webb, Krzyst of Ziarek, Enrique Dussell, Juan Carlos Scannone, Lamberto Schuurman, J. F. Goud and Josef Wohlmuth. These thinkers have built up and reconstructed specifically Christian themes such as divinity or God's grace under the scrutiny of Levinas' philosophy.

Third, a collection of thinkers have outlined a new structure by which theology can be understood, or indeed a re-conceptualization of the theological task itself. This list includes Jean-Louis Chrétien, Stephen Curkpatrick and Jean-Luc Marion. Notably, this list is shorter and each of these theorists has profound interests in philosophy as well as in theology. Theirs is the development of a renewal of philosophical theology.

Interestingly, Horner believes the first approach to be the most difficult, largely because of the conceptual differences at play between philosophers and theologians. The metaphysical framework of many theologians pre-commits them to the kind of 'onto-theo-logy' that Levinas wishes to move beyond.[10] Horner notes that in the cases of both Michael Purcell and Michele Saracino, Levinas' conception of the content-less presence of God, arising in the face of the Other, appears to be incorporated directly into their work. It is not that either accepts an uncritical theological appropriation of Levinas, but that the full sway of consequences this appropriation may result in have not been pursued. Such a consideration can be seen in the development of their work. Nevertheless, in both cases there is present an attempt to push a dialogue between Levinas and another great mind as far as it might go, in Karl Rahner and Bernard Lonergan, respectively. In the case of Rahner, the transcendence afforded to the human subject in the awakening to grace offers a trajectory that can meet the Levinasian condition for an authentic ethics.[11] Purcell notes that Levinas' condition relies on the God who arises in the awakening to the Other. This God remains empty of definable content, but makes possible the infinity of the other person whose alterity demands an ethical responsibility. It is not the case that Rahner's supernatural existential coincides with the alterity in the face of the Other, but the transcendental possibilities of Rahner's approach appear to move in the direction that Levinas intends. In other words, one must follow the logic of Levinas and theological interlocutors to see how their dialogue is fruitful. Purcell describes a situation in which the natural relation of the human person to the world is already a witness to the awakening to grace, in which '[n]aturality and supernaturality are entwined'.[12] In this way, the comparison of Levinas to specific theologians can indeed be fruitful, but the location of those points at which philosophically and theologically conceived conceptualizations are incompatible is equally important.

As can be seen, a number of thinkers appear in more than one list, notably the first and the second. This displays the relatively early stages in which theological studies of Levinas are taking place, such that various approaches are being tested and re-evaluated. In the second list, Horner highlights the work of Roger Burggraeve. His contribution to interpreting Levinas has been highly significant, especially for the use of the Bible and the development of a scriptural ethics. For Burggraeve, both the Bible and the Talmud are important sources in indicating the way that ethics is of 'our very essence'.[13] By using these sources, he promotes a coincidence of the biblical notion of love with the insistently complete responsibility that shapes Levinas' ethics. In this way, a love-ethic develops that is entirely concerned with the appearance of the Other in need and privation. Burggraeve offers a deeply engaging perseverance in working out the logic of Levinas' philosophy. He argues that the ethical content of the face-to-face is a transcendent moment of radically subversive consequences. In fact, the presence of God – the thought that rises in the face-to-face moment – allows the possibility of witnessing the glory and the height of the Other. It is subversive in the sense that its ethical content exceeds all other impositions of the socioeconomic and political orders; even those intended to proffer justice.[14] For Burggraeve, the face-to-face *is* the moment of human–divine encounter, in the sense that a divine encounter cannot take place otherwise. Levinas' subjectivity holds this in constant sight and makes it possible to speak of an ethics that surpasses every other ethical encounter. It is not to reject the legitimacy of institutions and juridical frameworks *per se*, but rather to insist that they are radically contingent upon the inter-subjectivity of the concrete transcendence of the face-to-face. Of course, this remains paradoxical, in that Levinas' inter-subjectivity relies on incarnate presence, even as he privileges the transcendence of a God who arises in the face-to-face moment. Burggraeve views this move as a paradoxically immanent transcendence, in which God calls from the face of the other a responsible response in the oneself. The depths to which this call reaches are great, but they call the oneself out of itself to seek out the good in the Other, which in turn is both transcendent and infinite in its interior dimension.

It can be seen that Levinas' language depends constantly on the power of paradoxical imagery to convey his thought. The height of the Other is illustrated by reference to interior depths. For Burggraeve, the theology at work makes the human other a religious creature, whose religiosity is that of being inspired by the 'Infinite, the Good', and it is the condition of ethics.[15] Here, God is equivalent to the infinite and the good and is, therefore, the activity of liberation in the face of the Other. This being so, an equivalence is reached between God and the act of liberation, such that ethical responsibility seeks out and is driven by a demand that has already taken place in the face-to-face. God has issued the demand and responsible action is a participation in the demand for justice that has already begun in the face. The event of liberation begins not with the response to the Other, but in the epiphany of the face-to-face, which is to make God Himself the liberating event. God arises as a thought, and he is present in the epiphany of the face.

This brings us to further reflection on the third way in which theologians have responded to Levinas. The restructuring of theology or reshaping of its nature as a task is of particular importance. Horner takes up the work of Jean-Luc Marion, whose thought she has done much to promote and interpret. Marion is both a philosopher and a theologian, and in both respects he relies substantially upon Levinas to develop his unique approach. Horner identifies three crucial facets that situate both Levinas and Marion's work within the same broad trajectory.[16]

The first facet is Levinas' displacement of onto-theology. By his attempt to think 'otherwise than being', Levinas opens the way for Marion to think through meaning without the category of Being as such.[17]

The second facet is Levinas' turn to the signification of the other person. The appearance of the Other usurps all other categories and limitations, standing insistently and irreducibly. In reflecting on this signification, Marion has a structure that informs his own phenomenology of, respectively, the icon, the face, and love. In each of these, the signification of the Other carries an intentionality which names the self through a 'call' that accomplishes a 'counter-intentionality' that saturates one's intuitive capacity.[18] The Other is a superlative presence that makes possible Marion's description of the relation between the oneself and these other phenomena.

The third facet is the Levinasian injunction of the face, 'Thou shalt not kill', which for Marion is the 'call' or the 'appeal'.[19] In the call of the face, the oneself is addressed in a singular demand. One receives the address as a demanding excess of meaning in which both a summons and a command are issued without hesitation. Marion takes this up in his phenomenological analysis of what he describes as 'saturated phenomena' (the event, the idol, flesh and the icon).[20] The call and the appeal, which is received in a presence that exceeds all understanding and containment, which 'saturates' one's intentionality, relies very much on the first two facets. Levinas' critique of Western philosophy and its compulsion to circumvent all thought into Being, and the ethical signification of alterity in the face of the Other, together create a means by which this third facet operates. The otherness of the Other, who is thought beyond Being, is present in a way that so saturates one's ethical relationship with its subjective constitution that it, in effect, envelopes and overcomes the oneself. This effectively denies the possibility of reducing the Other, even if in practical terms the other may be diminished in its phenomenal experience.

The appearing of such another person in this way is the stuff of concrete human experience. It must not be interpreted as a mystical experience in any overtly religious sense, but as the ethical content that rises in the subjectivity of the most urbane of human encounters. It is a radicalization of human sociality. Marion takes this human moment – seemingly banal in its domestic sensibility – and interprets it to allow for the possibility of revelation. As Horner describes, revelation may have a content, although as an excessive content it is defined by the 'inevitable supplement of a hermeneutics'.[21] In other words, the excess has a boundary experience in which interpretation is necessitated. In this way, Marion sees in Levinas a means of conceiving revelation as a phenomenological opportunity. Revelation is an event that also exceeds human experience, yet it also has a content that is open to philosophical scrutiny. This is obviously indebted to Levinas, but achieves something he would not have necessarily endorsed, which is an imaginative and energetic relationship between philosophy and theology. In this perspective, theology cannot help but be present just as the thought of God arises in the epiphany of the Other.

However, discordance can be found in Levinas' work. For example, David Bentley Hart has argued that Levinas' account of the Other relies on an account of the 'ethical sublime' that disenfranchises the unique beauty of the other person.[22] He sees in Levinas such a perfect sublimity in the absolute character of alterity, that the authentically *other* person effectively disappears. The absolute otherness of the Other denies a meeting of the face-to-face, because it persists in rendering other that which is also particular, unique and utterly present. In this way, Hart views in Levinas a problematic rendering of alterity, by which an incarnate motivation to love is made impossible. The Other is always too out of reach, always a deferred presence who resides in a sublime intensity of ethical provocation. Hart fears the results of Levinas' account of such an Other who must necessarily become a 'persecutor', a 'sacrificer of hostages', an 'accuser' and a 'stranger to gratitude' who makes the oneself a hostage to alterity.[23] For Hart, this is a reduction of the Other to a banal ethical category which is essentially inhuman, or more precisely, dehumanized. The Incarnation, for Hart, is an affirmation of the uniqueness of each particular moment of incarnate of love, of individuated bodies and their faces. Hart, therefore, defends a position of vast distance between Levinas' ethics and a theological ethics of otherness.

Here, Hart identifies a problematic area of Levinasian thought. If Levinas' Other is not conceived as an authentic human experience of flesh and blood, then the signification of the presence of the Other becomes a formal category without an embodied content. The notion of the face is the clearest point of contention here, because Levinas claims strikingly that the face is not an appearance but a non-appearance. It is the very epiphany of alterity described in terms of an absolute distance. And if the Other is merely the ghostly formality of an ethical construct, then the ethical response to such an alterity becomes further disengaged from the horizon of the possible. This is identified by John Milbank, who criticizes an approach that envisions the highest exemplification of the good to consist in sacrificial death on behalf of an Other or others.[24] Milbank views Levinas in this group, as well as Jan Patocka, Jacques Derrida and, in a limited way, Jean-Luc Marion. He outlines four foundational elements to this approach. The first is an understanding of the gift that is perfected by a denial of any counter-gift. That is, *giving* is only truly a moment of *gifting* if it is characterized by self-sacrifice, otherwise it hides in its hand the structure of a contractual agreement. Second, death is conceived as the circumstance in which ethical action is possible. This is so because death makes us intrinsically vulnerable creatures, and so ethics has a serious life-threatening gravity to it. Furthermore, a readiness to die for the Other proves the sincere disinterest of the ethical gesture, thus precluding the will to power. Third, it is assumed that the self becomes self-aware and aware of other people by the cry of the vulnerable and the consequence that one must sacrifice oneself to meet the need indicated by that cry. The Other, therefore, is greater than us, and so the notion of God appears. Fourth, Milbank argues that the ontology presented in this schema ensures that the world is stripped of a divine presence that stands apart or over the category of death. Moreover, the human other is interpreted outside of the integrity of humanity such that neither God nor the human person is present as such. As Milbank puts it, God is 'reduced to a shadow of the human other', and so the death of the self for the other person becomes a moment of ultimate significance.[25] Death is the revelation and the definer of that which is ethical, and there is no God to temper or explain the nature of the ethical imperative.[26]

Milbank offers an important theological rejoinder to Levinas' account of otherness, because much of the latter's own ethics follows the four elements Milbank describes. Indeed, Milbank acknowledges the consistency of this approach and implicitly recognizes the appeal of logic at work. He recognizes that in both Levinas' and others' contemporary account of ethics, as well as his own, is the contested topic of what it is to seek out the good in morality. In the giving of a gift, Milbank finds it difficult to defend the notion that the content of the gift is of no significance, as if the formal exchange is the only defining feature of the event. After all, a pure disinterest, if it is conscious, must assuredly result in some level of satisfaction in the mind of the giver, simply on the basis of being aware that what is being pursued is a model of gift-giving that privileges disinterest. To overcome this, the gift-receiver would have to be anonymous, and furthermore the gift would have to be content-less. Milbank rightly contends that the kind of absurd levels of self-sacrificing purity that such an approach maintains are unsustainable if not impossible.

Milbank, therefore, suggests that a better notion of the good would be an image defended by Robert Spaemann, that of the feast.[27] In this, the rich do not give to the poor in a moment of absolute self-abnegation, but instead, both sit together in what Milbank calls their 'convivial interaction'.[28] The one who first gives does not deny his or her own self in desolation, because he or she partakes also of the feast. The image is stronger still, because rather than pitch one person against another in an assumed ontological violence, it takes up the fullness of Being as the occasion of festive sociality, in which a multitude of participants take what is plentiful and have their fill. Milbank bases this on his reading of the resurrection of Christ, in whom a promise is pledged of heavenly reward in which feasting is a primary event. In the resurrection, gift-giving is not conceived as utter self-sacrifice, but as a reconciling moment in which inter-subjectivity continually develops in the light of an ontology of the good. The lost and the injured have their place at the table of the resurrection, in which an infinity of cordial community is manifested not simply as some kind of eschatological hope, but by virtue of a limited participation in a present form. Both Hart and Milbank not only identify the problematic rendering of the Other in Levinas, but also engage it with a robust theological description of alterity conceived in a Christian paradigm. For both, the ethics of responsibility are just as demanding, but it in turn is provoked not simply by the need of the Other, but by a promise of shared company in the feast, in which the goods of the earth are warmly nourishing and enjoyed. In this way, Milbank avoids what he calls an 'impersonal totality', and calls upon a theological response that might correct a Levinasian vision not only with the substance of faith, but also with the substantive promise of the fulfilment of faith: 'To give, to be good, is already to be resurrected'.[29] For Milbank and others, there remains a necessity for a valid onto-theology that allows for this vision of the good in the light of God's prior act. It does not erase responsibility, but situates it within a broader arc of giving and receiving.

And so the question must be asked, if theology is possible after Levinas, despite these criticisms, what kind of shape will it have? Critics of Levinas have argued that his account of the Other is inherently disincarnate, and that onto-theology remains an essential means of conceiving the world theologically. The problem of the disincarnate Other is identified by Terry Eagleton as 'something oppressively inhuman'. . . 'whose fleshly presence is more an intimidatory law than a ground of friendship'.[30] It has been shown how a number of positive responses have been made, from dialogues between his thought and major theologians, to Levinasian integration with specific theological themes, and finally to a new structure or conception of theology. It is proposed that this final way of responding to Levinas is a necessary help to theology itself. Levinas disturbs theology, not as one who uncovers decaying foundations and unreliable pillars, but as one who discovers the poor man in the dark and wakes him up with warm clothes and food. The provocation of Levinas is such that the poverty of one's own position is unmasked, not for the sake of public humiliation, but for moving past facades and healing the fragile body one finds. Thus, the presence of theology is already given in the epiphany of the Other; the gift of an ethical vocation. Such a presence, if it is to be enacted responsibly, will require some clarity about how such a vocation might be performed. In this respect, a number of themes are highlighted by Levinas that aid in his provocation of theology as an ethical task. One of them is prayer.

Theology as *prayer*. This is a controversial mutual identification of terms. It has a long history and one could begin with the biblical demand that disciples 'pray without ceasing' (1 Thes 5:17). There are many prayers in both the Hebrew Scriptures and the New Testament, containing a great number of themes, styles and contexts. It is clear that prayer is not altogether easy and so the Spirit of God is implored to complete imperfect prayers: 'For we do not know what to pray for as we ought, but the Spirit himself intercedes for us with groanings too deep for words' (Rom 8:26). Of course, a person hopes that his or her prayer will be a sweet experience of pure delight, such as that described in the psalm, 'Let my prayer be counted as incense before you' (Ps 141:2). Yet prayer, the giving over of one's soul to God, is often the arduous territory of despair and anxiety. Even in this example, the prayer itself is that what is given to God might be *received* as incense, not *necessarily* experienced by the pray-er as sweet to the nostrils. It is no accident that Christ saw a need to teach his disciples to pray, and to specify a form of words that would act as both a set prayer to recite and a format in which other prayer is be interpreted (Matt 6:9-13; Lk 11:2-4). The Lord's Prayer – the *Our Father* or *Pater Noster* in its Latin liturgical tradition – remains one of the few liturgical texts common to the Christian tradition. Because it is given in two of the four Gospel narratives of the New

Testament, it is a prayer that properly belongs to all Christians, regardless of other differences. It places the disciple in a context of humility before God, and formally expresses the self-effacing contingency in which one lives. Specifically, the person who prays seeks out from the divine Other all that is necessary in terms of one's 'daily bread' and the radical forgiveness that renews one's relationship to God and to other people. The deliverance from evil is situated only after one's contingency is attested to, and so one's personal salvation in an intrinsically unethical world follows the prayerful renewal of relationships and material need. The awareness of evil, expressed in the prayer itself, shows the importance of having one's eyes open to both God and the world. In a sense, theology begins in the context of such a prayer. For St Augustine, we ought not pray for what we need, because God already knows.[31] Rather, prayer is given as a means by which we may increase our desire for God, and be better prepared for his blessings to us. Desire for God is both the content and the objective of prayer. More recently, Hans Urs von Balthasar encourages a 'theology on one's knees'.[32] In this sense, prayer is the originary theology, for it is the humble response to God's first initiative. There are many other examples, but suffice it to say that the association of authentic God-talk – theology – with authentic prayer is a recurring theological theme.

How does Levinas' account of God and the ethics of alterity relate to prayer? In an essay called *Prayer Without Demand*, Levinas interprets prayer philosophically in response to the suffering of the Other.[33] It is a short essay, but dense in its interpolation of theological and philosophical consequences. It deserves some attention, and indeed opens a way to relate his account of the religiosity of the human person and God to ethics. Levinas draws on the Jewish Rabbinic tradition, especially a work by Rabbi Hayyim Volozhiner (1759–1821) called *Nefesh ha'Hayyim* [Soul of Life], which is probably a reference to Gen. 2:7 and God's breath in the life of Adam. Rabbi Volozhiner was himself a pupil of Elijah Gaon of Vilna

(1720–97), a Lithuanian scholar of both the Talmud and the Kabbalah, and whose biblical knowledge outshone his peers. Both Rabbis were committed to a Talmudic form of Judaism, which was deeply suspicious of the religious enthusiasm of Hasidism in Eastern Europe and any reduction of holy texts to mysticism. For these Talmudists, the Torah provided the content of the heart of their religious culture, in which a self-confident display of Judaism resisted the modernist enlightenment themes of Gentile Europe. Rabbinic scholarship saw in the study of the Torah and Talmudic commentaries a discipline that, in Levinas' words, 'reaches heights as lofty as those of liturgy, surpassing even the transports of prayer'.[34] Levinas contends that this tradition could not do without worship or rituals, but it nevertheless emphasizes the vocation of Israel to put into practice not only a pious behaviour in response to God's commandments, but also a philosophy of life derived from those same commands. For Levinas, the legislative texts of the *Halakhah* (rules which come from both biblical and Talmudic writings) already indicate a derivative, or implicit 'philosophical system' that is distinctively Jewish.[35] For Levinas, the book called *Nefesh ha'Hayyim*, which was published posthumously, is an example of such a philosophy that, while shaped immutably by Rabbinic and Jewish scholarship, is also a fundamental account of reality for all persons.[36] While the work is devotional, it is, in a sense, also metaphysical and of concern to ethical thought outside strictly Jewish faith and practice.

Levinas takes from Rabbi Hayyim Volozhiner's work some important notions. He sees in it the opening of perspectives on the 'fundamental structure of Judaism, the religion of Study and the Law'.[37] It is notable that for Levinas, the dual activities of both 'Study' and the 'Law' have a religious dimension. It is not simply that religion has its scholastic and legalistic aspects or consequences, or even expressions, but that the work of scholarship and the law, in themselves, are religious. In such a view, all aspects of the world are interpreted in the light of religion, because all things derive their existence from an infinite source. Furthermore, the world – or 'worlds' – are radically contingent upon the divine energy which permits their ongoing existence.[38] The various creatures that exist, referred to as worlds, owe to God not only their creation but also the breath that maintains their material and spiritual integrity. Each of these worlds participates in a hierarchy of being, at the peak of which is found the throne of God. God's energy emanates through each successive world, by which a mediation of that power is shared with the next hierarchical layer. This will not be an unusual image for a reader of the Kabbalah, but Levinas interprets in the Rabbi's account of this hierarchy a complication when it comes to the human person. While the human creature is made from the substance that exists at the lowest level of this hierarchy – the flesh formed in the shadow of the divine that makes up the body – it is also the creature whose soul rightly sits alongside God at the top of the hierarchy. In the body, the human person must operate at the level of 'doing' and of 'work', but in the spiritual faculty of the mind, humanity alone can either condition (positively), or disturb or block (negatively) the association of God with the world. That is, the soul must act through the body in perfect freedom; either obeying God's word and fulfilling the divine law so that all creation might be intimately connected with God, or work through the body to disturb or even block God's word in the world. In this way, all other creatures, indeed all creation, look to the human person and place their hope in humanity's fulfilment of the law. The human person then does not sit easily at one point in the hierarchy, but acts in a dynamically unsettled way as an arbiter of either God's peace or an interruption of God's presence in the world; the human person exists at both extreme poles. The burden of this responsibility is absolutely tremendous. It means that every particular act, thought or word is of fundamental importance to the constitution of creation in relation to its creator. Levinas quotes Volozhiner, who says of the human person that, 'not one detail of his acts, of his words and of his thoughts is ever lost'.[39] This could only be received happily by a saint who does no harm. For those of us who are not saints, this ought to make us tremble, for it indicates that every wicked thought is consequential, though we might wish to forget them.Volozhiner could see clearly that the result of this conceptualization of the world is a great focus upon the subjective experience of the human person. He speaks of its influence upon the man who understands this, that his heart will be fearful and he will tremble at how far one small misdeed might reach in effecting corruption and destruction in the world.

Of course, this situation cannot simply be explained as a form of distributed or collective responsibility. It is not that each person owns a small share in a greater significance of general responsibility. Levinas interprets the hierarchy to mean that each person is fundamentally responsible for all other creatures and it, therefore, is the means of interpreting its own self-identity. Man, for Levinas, is indeed made in the image of God (Gen. 1:27), but is also shown to be a 'living soul' (after the meaning of Gen. 2:7). Levinas also connects this with the words of Isaiah 51:16, in which the laying of God's foundations of the earth is given to the mouth of man.[40] Levinas continually seizes on these demanding biblical words to exploit the greatest possible ethical content from them. He sees in the Bible, as in Volozhiner's thought, an insistent responsibility that is given to each human person, by which the being or non-being of the universe depends. This illustrates two lessons for Levinas.[41] First, God's humility is demonstrated in the handing over of such responsibility to humanity. Such a humble action perhaps also shows the greatness of God. Second, this radically inverts the relationship between ontology and ethics. In Levinas' reading of these texts, being (*être*) is shown to lack the ability to provide beings (*étants*) with an 'adequate *raison d'être*'.[42] Being *qua* being can offer no provocation to pursue the good, or indeed explain in any adequate language the structure or purpose of living authentically. Indeed, it cannot answer the question of what authenticity might be. This is a prime example of the way in which Levinas' philosophy and his Talmudic reading mutually confirm and endorse each other. The philosophical development articulated in both *Totality and Infinity* and *Otherwise than Being* finds here ready endorsement in Levinas' reading of both Scripture and a particular rabbinic text. Fundamentally, for him, Being itself is not to be put aside, but reinterpreted in the light of the ethical demand contained in Scripture. In the hierarchy explained above, the 'intelligibility of being' becomes possible only when ethics is the point at which philosophy begins.[43] Humanity then has a responsibility to irrupt into being by living for all others. Other creatures, and especially human creatures, are the motivating factor by which one can act for the sake of God's presence in the world. The continuance of the world depends then on the smallest of measures, of a love described by Levinas as the 'first value', the dwindled amount of humanity left in existence.[44] God's association is revealed in the most disinterested of human activities, of thoughts, words and actions that endorse the other person in a world of divine emanations. Acts of love which remain hidden and discrete are, perhaps, the most powerful acts of all, and upon which the whole universe depends.

A further connection is made between Hayyim Volozhiner's account of the world and with Levinas' own account of being-for-the-other. While Volozhiner's rabbinic vision is locally and particularly realized by virtue of its theological framework in the Torah, the Talmud and the Kabbalah, Levinas argues that the ethical vision is not limited to Judaism. Precisely because of the universal dimension of human responsibility in a hierarchy of being, which precedes Being itself, Levinas views an ethical structure which belongs to every person. The experience of humanity is such that the multiple worlds of creaturely subjectivity with which humans interact issue a demand that being-for-others precedes any notion of being-for-itself. For Levinas, the biblical reference to such themes is universal and not limited to the people of Israel. Injustice, according to Psalm 82:5, shakes 'all the foundations of the earth'. So, the

Jewish Scriptures and other holy texts within that tradition open themselves to a universalizing philosophy of ethics for the Other. This brings the present discussion to the way in which prayer operates integrally to such categories.

Jewish piety envisages the creation of the just person, or, the one who truly prays and acts justly. For Volozhiner, the process by which the human person acts justly in obedience to God's word and relates creation to its Creator, is profoundly enacted in the *true prayer*. This cannot be understood apart from Levinas' vision of the hierarchy above, in which one's soul is elevated to the level of God, whereas one's body acts and works at the lowest point of the hierarchy. Human materiality is, thus, a mediation for spirituality, which is the emanation of God's light closest to God Himself. Prayer is a means in which the whole person, body and soul participates authentically in the just work of acting for others. But what is prayer? Levinas does not describe its essence but its practice: 'Prayer never asks for anything for oneself; strictly speaking, it makes no demands at all, but is an elevation of the soul'.[45] In other words, prayer is an elevation to contemplation of the divine face. Prayer is action experienced in the extreme passivity of one who rises to contemplation before the divine face. It is not, for Levinas, the objective content of a textual form or even of a liturgical canon. For him, prayer is the highest *imago* of a true ethics, not so much religious as it is 'religion'.[46] Alternatively, the event of prayer is itself an icon of the true. To be sure, the contemplative moment must be effected in a self-emptying of the self – the being-for-others described above – in which experiencing the presence of the Other is possible. God's association with the worlds of creatures and creatureliness depends on this moment of authentic prayerful self-emptying. The love of the oneself for God must be a complete love or it is a diminishment of the soul. Indeed, the biblical image of one's soul being poured out for God (see especially Deut 6:5) is invoked to emphasize the abject self-emptying that true prayer necessitates. In such an account, the body and the soul are made distant from each other, which for Volozhiner is the letting go of a weighty and vain encumbrance between humanity and God. Levinas uncritically incorporates into his thought the anti-bodily prejudice of Volozhiner, and sees in the rising of the soul the essence of the ethical. Prayer is the spiritual surrender to God and the detachment of the self from Being. If there is any delight in this passive surrender, it is God's alone. Levinas quotes Proverbs 15:8: 'the prayer of the upright is his delight'. The just man prays justly and therefore acts justly, resulting in the fulfilment of God's hope for an association with the worlds. It is important to critically acknowledge that Levinas is too susceptible in the account here of the body–soul distinction. It is not a healthy distinction, but one that stretches the human person across a hierarchy of being in which authenticity and in-authenticity sit at each extremity. This is an anthropology that bears a Manichean distrust of the human body, without the hope of either a Gnostic letting go or of the Christian faith in a bodily resurrection. Because of this, its broad implication is a negative reading of the body. It is a philosophy that avoids the place of bodily or en-fleshed 'sense' in ethical knowledge.[47] The hierarchy of being assumes too quickly the lower place of the body both in its historical experience and in its future *telos*. A fuller, integrated account of the somatic experience of the human person would challenge Levinas' interpretation and counter it by appealing to the fundamentally embodied nature of the human person in the realm of religious experience. The one who prays and seeks to integrate prayer into his or her life is one who engages a different posture with the body, and whose mind is motivated to attend to the practices and habits of the body. Nevertheless, what Levinas does achieve is a challenge towards the idea that prayer is purely personal or that it is merely a communicative tool between divinity and humanity. In Levinas' reading of his own tradition, the world/s themselves depend on a simple act of prayer.

Following this, the worlds are not simply unleashed to go on in existence, as if being itself was adequate. Levinas states the rather more surprising notion that God 'needs prayer', just as fidelity to the Torah is required for the world's 'existence and elevation' to be made possible in God's association with them.[48] It is unclear how strong a point Levinas wishes to make concerning God's own need for authentic prayer. His use of the term is partially rhetorical in that it moves his argument along without overemphasization, but it does reveal something of the way in which the term God is only used by him in terms of ethics. It may simply serve the philosopher's need to upset established assumptions and challenge the status quo of the uncritically religious observer. After all, what is essential for Levinas is not God or the being of God or even Being as such, but of being-for-others.

The emphasis on prayer allows for a coincidence of what is hoped for with what is enacted in ethical responsibility. Faced with a world of worlds and various levels of a hierarchy of being, the human person must shirk the natural inclination to pray demandingly for justice, and instead pray *without* demand, allowing one's ethics to be enacted *as* the hope for others. Faced with being, the contemplation of God opens to the ethical horizon. In these terms, the passivity of the human person cannot conclude in that moment, but allow for the more insistent practice of responsibility to intervene. One seeks out the salvation of others with such an insistence. As Levinas says, the 'ethical must intervene!'[49]

Levinas recognizes that the liturgical prayers of modern Judaism derive from the replacement of the daily sacrifices made in the (now destroyed) temple.[50] They are not prayers without a history, and in fact were largely designed to institute a new liturgical order not bound to the burnt offerings (or holocausts) presented prior to the temple's destruction. These sacrifices were meant to be perfect and complete, offered up in utter abnegation to the flames. Given that a burnt offering of flesh is no longer called for, Levinas reflects further on the nature of his 'prayer without demand', such that the sacrifice must necessarily be an interior one for the human person. The glory of God is honoured by such prayers, and despite Levinas' injunction to resist the desire to make demands, he takes up the Talmud's authorization of some individual supplications. Yet even here, they are circumvented within the more significant order of prayer as contemplation before God's presence. The Talmud does allow for such supplications, but only when Israel as a whole is in danger or when its people are persecuted and held in contempt. Levinas accepts the theological dimension of the teaching; that the people of Israel are not to be nationalistic in priority but are bearers of revelation. The revelation of God comes first. And this revelation, even in the names it gives itself, remains always a certain enigma before his people, as if even the statement, 'The Holy One, blessed be He', does not promise perfect disclosure.[51] If God's people are so under siege that the ongoing witness and proclamation of that revelation is threatened, then prayer for oneself is to be offered. At the very point of suffering, God's name is invoked and his own presence re-situates suffering in relation to his will. At this juncture – the experience of suffering – prayer becomes a participation in God.

Levinas provides here a means of envisaging theology *as* prayer. The just one who suffers calls upon the name of God and sits within an entirely different category than that of the one who prays only for one's own happiness. It must be remembered that in the point made above, Levinas connects the meaning of prayer with God's need of prayers for the sake of relation with the worlds. And not only for the sake of relation, but also for the world's very existence, in which the various creatures experience their contingency in relation to divinity. Levinas describes the presence of God prior to the phenomenon of human suffering: 'God, prior to any demand, is already there with me'.[52] Scripture attests to God's presence to the one who suffers in his name (Levinas notes Ps 91:15 and Is 63:9). The suffering person prays on behalf of the God who suffers through humanity's transgression and through the suffering by which that transgression is expiated. That is to say, God humbles Himself to allow some role in the suffering person of an expiatory suffering, or of a suffering *for* others. The suffering of God is always an excess which cannot be comprehended or described in full. The orisons offered on human lips find meaning in the suffering of the God who makes prayer possible. Because divine suffering exceeds human suffering, the individual human person who suffers is lightened of its load, 'his own suffering diminished', and the comparison between God's suffering and human suffering lessens the burden for human persons.[53] This aspect of Levinas' account is not explained in full. In what way does God suffer at all, let alone suffer in an excess compared to human suffering? Levinas holds that the bitterness of God's suffering sweetens human suffering, but again, one might ask in what way? The denial of participation (described elsewhere in this book) seems to be overturned at this point, and God Himself becomes the possibility for expiatory suffering. Christian theology holds that in Christ, this is precisely what God achieves, yet the way in which Levinas makes this connection is not clear. Perhaps the answer is to be found in the word 'immediately', with which Levinas connects the suffering of an 'I' with God's suffering.[54] Levinas assumes a contiguous occasion of suffering between the oneself and the divine Other that displaces time. The prayer of the suffering self immediately suggests a divine suffering preceding the *chronos* of the world, and it must be remembered that for Levinas, the world depends on the ethical/prayerful interaction between existence and God. The intersecting moment of the human person who abnegates its own self for the sake of God is itself a suffering; one that coincides with the God who first suffers. In other words, the prayer of the one who suffers occasions a time before time and before the self and, furthermore, it precedes the existence of the world. It must also be recalled that in Levinas' reading of Volozhiner's text, scholarship itself reaches the very heights of prayer. In this reading of Levinas' own account of suffering, it can be seen that theology, if it remains radically disposed to the divine law, is itself an example of the prayer envisaged by Levinas. Theology is radically committed to God, not in the form of a *praxis*, but in a contemplative moment of self-kenosis. Furthermore, because it is a self-abnegation that bears itself up to God as the first cause, it is a primary experience of suffering-for-the-other. To theologize is to suffer. Theology, as a subjective experience for each of its practitioners, opens itself to God and seeks to intersect the authentic experience of the divine with the creatureliness of the world. Other persons, especially in their suffering, become an opportunity to act faithfully and sustain the world's existence by participation in that small measure of love of which Levinas speaks. The rabbinic tradition that Levinas interprets, of scholarly rigour framed by sacred texts, becomes also an ethical vision in which prayer and theology operate at the same level within being. Indeed, theology as prayer accentuates an *exemplar* of being-for-others, and the prayer of the suffering person becomes a foundational event for the continuing narrative of the world.

Now, the account of theology as prayer requires a fierce commitment both to the task of theology alongside others and as an approach towards the divine that issues no demands. It is, in effect, the duality of an activity of excursion coupled with a sincere passivity. Yet despite its dual nature, it constitutes one and the same action of responding appropriately to the event of alterity. Roger Burggraeve refers to the need for a 'radical alterity' to save the 'I'.[55] He argues that all subjective experience requires the event of a personal disposition of sovereignty for salvation or liberation to be concretized. He takes from Levinas the description of the *il y a* – the 'there is' – of human being, as carrying a disturbing dynamic of calamity.[56] That is, the essential beginning point for a philosophical anthropology is the existential problem of the substance of experience in the present moment. Indeed, this is Levinas at his most existential, although he does not see the need to reject the notion of essence as such. Rather, the basic state of being for the human person is envisaged as a kind of *actus essendi*, in which all acting is to be interpreted and understood. It is a manifestation that is never static or unmoving, and continues to unfold its own being as a 'there is' that is always beginning and always becoming. The calamity that Levinas perceives in the human person is the event of being which seeks to discover itself through itself, in effect turning a dynamic event into a self-enclosure of repetition and ultimately fragmentation. Burggraeve defends Levinas' account as having a positive dimension, in that the self-recurrence of the self holds the positive possibility of constituting a certain mastery within its own freedom to 'become', such that a departure from the self towards the self is a continual possibility.[57] While self-recurrence must ultimately be broken so that the oneself may be interrupted by the needful Other, it remains the case that persons are free to discover themselves anew in a kind of self-recreation. It is not complete, but it is nevertheless an example of authenticating action. The theologian who conceives theology as prayer has embarked not on a mystical endeavour as such, but rather on the movement of authenticity that Burggraeve calls 'the salvation of the intramundane' 'in contrast to calamity'.[58]

Prayer is indeed a spiritual activity, and Christian theology has access to resources that emphasize this time and again. But the banalities of the everyday become a locus in which the cross and the resurrection are enlivening categories for an authentic *actus essendi* that is truly oriented towards the Other. Such a theological task is humble and ultimately suspicious of those theologies that would circumvent the world at hand. It certainly begins with an openness to the light that penetrates the darkness (see Jn 1:5), but in self-abnegation seeks out the refraction of that light in the banal and the mundane. It must necessarily remain open to the miraculous and the other-worldly if it is to receive the gifts of faith, but not seek them out as prizes to be won. The reduction of faith to such things overlooks the suffering faces that line the street, hidden and invisible in plain sight. A hagiographic example of the task of theologian in this light comes from St Thomas Aquinas.[59] One tradition has it that a particularly prayerful nun had become famous for levitation. Many came to see her and marvelled at this miraculous gift of holiness. Thomas grew interested and visited her household. He knocked and entered. And soon enough, he witnessed the woman majestically float up the stairwell without use of limbs or ropes. Whereas everyone else gaped in amazement, Thomas looked on bored and unimpressed. He was asked to indicate his response, and so he looked up and exclaimed, 'my what big feet you have'. He then left and, presumably, returned to his study. Thomas took no interest in the spectacular that glittered like a trophy adorning reality. Rather, he wished to perceive being in its dynamic exigencies, and so framed his work theologically such that wisdom and revelation might both touch upon a description of the world. In doing so, he avoided the other extreme, in which theology becomes subsumed by an ethics that would reconstruct the world itself in terms of an immediate notion of justice or the good. No, an adequate theological ethics, informed by Levinas, is also suspicious of politics and statist intervention. An ethics of care that reduces itself to formal structures would have the air of liberation, but not the excess of loving intentionality that the suffering other calls for, nor the excess of self-giving that an event like Incarnation makes possible. In this way, it better honours a theology with a capacity to liberate, rather than a liberation theology as such.

Levinas' work unsettles foundations and presuppositions. Philosophy is unsettled by his accusation that it has overlooked the otherness of the Other and requires radically new directions. Furthermore, the interruption of ethics as first philosophy does not only unsettle, but also provokes a theological response. This occurs because of Levinas' linking of the notion of God with the epiphany of the other person. Levinas disturbs the slumber of theology and causes it to awake to its ethical responsibility in a kind of sobering up. As Levinas puts it, 'a wakefulness on the eve of a new awakening, Ethics'.[60] Such sobering up in the act of waking causes theology to blink into the light and collect its thoughts, but it cannot turn only to philosophical tools to return to such work; it must find those tools that are most suited to the work of the theologian. They include scripture, liturgy, proclamation, acts of mercy and a reorientation towards the Other who first makes theology possible. Fundamentally, it includes prayer. In this recollection of the task of theology and its ethical reawakening, a significant practice of self-recollection will take place. Much like the person who awakes suddenly and reaches for the glass of water, theology will replenish itself by inspecting carefully the fragments of words and actions from the evening before and by scrutinizing them from a penitential station. Indeed, a traumatic re-evaluation of its relationship with its own source-material requires a humble commitment to ongoing self-inspection, and an account of its relationship with philosophy. The festive posture outlined by Hart and Milbank gives testimony to this, for the act of penitence leads to joyful *communo* among others.

How then does Levinas help theology? It is argued that the provocation of Levinas is such that theology is awakened to the fact of the Other, and in so doing is awakened also to its own nakedness and shame. Theology finds itself looked upon in the event of alterity and receives the intentionality of the Other, which is a disturbance to the one who has stirred from a heavy slumber. As one who is looked upon by the Other, theology cannot shirk quietly into the shadows and hide its face, or at least not for long. The full glare of the light offers no dark reprieve, and theology refreshes itself in a shadow-less space in which, once again, it must enact an ethics of care for the Other. For all the ragged nakedness of theology, in which its weaknesses and failures are on display, it becomes clear that the Other continues to beckon in need. There is of course time for self-repair, but more immediate is the call of the Other who convicts the self with the urgent requirement to act. And so theology becomes once more not a system or a self-enclosed diction of its own concerns, but a *task*. As such, theology is exteriorly directed in the movement of ethical concern for the Other, orientated chiefly by the primary Other who first draws near and opens alterity up to a logic of love. That is to say, theology is an ethical endeavour in response to God. And that response begins in the contemplative moment described above. The coincidence of theology with prayer such that theology can be interpreted *as* prayer takes from Levinas the insight of the suffering one who prays. In the immediacy of experiencing the prayerful act of the suffering God, a non-chronological moment is announced. A time before time, in which God already participates alongside the human condition and actively holds together the integrity of creation, is envisaged. Lastly, this is an ethical vision that learns from Levinas that authentic prayer and authentic responsibility begin in the contemplation of God. This refuses then the diminishment of prayer (or indeed liturgy) and ethics, and holds them in a dramatic tension before the face of God.

Chapter 5

Preferring the Shadows: The 'Little Faith' of Israel

For Emmanuel Levinas, the faith of Israel is a 'little' faith.[1] He writes both as a philosopher and as a Talmudic commentator, because the littleness of the Jewish faith is, for him, a humble acceptance of a universal truth in the infinity of each particular moment. It is a littleness that strips the religious adherent of all vestige of power or moral authority, allowing he or she to act well for the suffering Other. It is a littleness that, paradoxically, results in a richness of moral activity that enables the rendering of justice in history. Furthermore, it is a littleness that allows Judaism to be shy of the world and its glories, and to turn quietly towards the rigours of study and prayer within its own textual inheritance. Rather than seeking greatness in the world through some false allure, it feels itself driven towards the holy lessons of its own Scriptures, from whence a true ethics of justice is derived. And in searching out the Scriptures to discover and re-learn its religious vocation, Judaism discovers the authenticating action of a holy reading. This kind of reading – both spiritual and intellectual – in which the moments of vagueness or confusion, or the contested texts of the tradition (from the Torah to contemporary Talmudic debate) demand careful argumentation and thought, results in a kind of domesticity of the texts which allows the Jewish man or woman to be at home within them even as they remain ambiguous. That is to say, in the textual home, which both inspires and provokes an ethical response, a person discovers the shadows of ambiguity. And in this context, Levinas prefers

97

the shadows of the holy texts than the glaring light of Western philosophy as it permeates the Gentile world.

Such a littleness among the shadows is counter-intuitive to a secular mindset, for which the religious must mean some form of stricture or imposition upon self-autonomy. This littleness is reflected in various ways across Levinas' texts, but its major themes will be viewed here as a theological possibility. For Levinas, the reading of Scriptures does not simply reveal a transcendent moment in which the thought of God is possible; it also enacts and concretizes transcendence. And the ambiguities themselves reveal the beauty of a God whose sheer simplicity is in his demand for justice. To express it more clearly, the reading of the texts is an event of transcendence. Levinas describes it thus:

> It suggests on the one hand that language, at the hour
> of its ethical truth – that is, of its full significance – is
> inspired, that it can therefore say more than it says,
> and that prophecy is thus not an act of genius, but the
> spirituality of the spirit expressing itself, the ability of
> human speech to extend beyond the primary intentions
> that carry it. This is perhaps possession by God, through
> which the idea of God comes to us.[2]

Here, Levinas is claiming something crucial about the nature of holy texts and their interpretation. He suggests that language, when it enters the service of ethics in its most concrete moments of action and response, offers an excess of meaning. Prophecy, therefore, has no claim of its own, but is the manner in which language reveals a spirituality, and expresses that spirituality in a fundamentally authentic excursion towards the receiver. It moves outside itself and transcends the present moment. This is a rare moment in which Levinas thinks of 'possession' by God in a positive light. Usually, Levinas is suspicious of the language of rapture or divine possession, but in this instance notes a liberating sense in which God might possess a person in an authentication of the truth. God is the supreme thought carried by language in the ethical moment, showing himself in the act of responsibility shown for others.

It is argued in this chapter that the theological resource of Levinas' approach to Judaism is in his retrieval of the relationship between the texts and the community of faith. He refuses any entrapment of Scriptures by the community, but rather insists upon a provocation in the texts that drives the faithful to study, ponder and reflect upon them more urgently. This is especially true of his Talmudic commentaries, and it would be a mistake to divorce them from his formal philosophical texts. While Levinas assumes a strong distinction between the two genres of writing, the influence of Talmudic thought and Jewish reflection on other writings is a necessary feature of his approach to alterity. In particular, it is here argued that Levinas' various writings both in the Talmudic tradition and in philosophy play a crucial role in determining the theological promise of the Levinasian project.

A case in point is the collection *Outside the Subject*, in which Levinas' essays from a range of contexts deal with the philosophy of other writers, including important Jewish philosophers from the twentieth century.[3] Figures such as Martin Buber and Franz Rosenzweig stand out for their crucial insights into the link between a Jewish intellectual framework and the structure of alterity. In fact, Levinas focuses on the strange event of reading a text in the light of contemporary critical exegesis of the Holy Scriptures. He defends a unique role for the act of faithful reading by viewing Scripture itself as a 'mode of being' that remains distinct from the 'pure matter' available to the analysis of the grammarian.[4] Here, he thinks of the Scriptures becoming stronger by their being stretched over the history of a lived tradition, much like the strings are stretched tautly over the wood of the violin. Beautiful music is played gently from the strength of those strings and the carved, treated wood that stands the test of time. In the same text, he speaks of the Bible as 'inhabited by a people', as if the Jews were, in effect, at home in the words and textual cadences of the Scriptures.[5] The Bible is not the bare words upon the pages, but a living context in which a particular people have developed their thought and their culture. It is in this common terrain of biblical language that Levinas pursues his conversation with those from whom he has learnt much, but with whom he disagrees. In Martin Buber, we have an example of a thinker whose association of divine alterity with the I-thou dynamic is respected, but reconstructed by Levinas. In Buber's major text on this theme, he argues for the alteration of a person as an 'It' towards a 'thou', predicated on language that derives from Jewish faith.[6] Buber holds in tension the *mysterium tremendum* of the God who appears but does not reveal his whole being, and whose power is invisible and yet permeates all creation, along with the self-presence of an utterly intimate divine personage, who knows the self better than the self. In Buber, the I-thou relationship is informed chiefly by an alterity that overcomes difference (but does not obliterate it) by drawing both together in mutual self-constitution. The self becomes more true to the self, and the Other becomes more authentically the other person, and in the between a communion of love conditions both in concrete community. For Levinas, the kind of reciprocity between the I and the thou is dismantled in favour of an irreducibly non-reciprocal relationship. For him, obligation towards the Other is inspired by the non-representable uniqueness of alterity. It is a proximity that upholds the accusatory reproach of the Other in his or her need, without reducing the self to obliteration. As Levinas argues, the Other refuses to be owned, 'falls to my responsibility, that is, signifies in all the ethical excellence of the obligation towards the Other, in fear for him or her, and love'.[7] Levinas, like Buber, employs terms that can be associated with God, as if the excellence once owed to God was now to be received in the en-fleshed presence of another human person. Levinas recognizes that in Buber, God is the intersecting moment in which all human relationships can derive their authentic meaning. Yet, as he admits, he is less certain that the 'Divine Person' resides in the 'Thou of dialogue' and that devotion and prayer are, in the end, 'dialogue' at all.[8] No, for Levinas, the close proximity of the divine is also a radical transcendence that stands over and above the self who acts. It is an idea that rises in a movement of glory, issuing a demand that remains absolute rather than shared and mediated. The Other is, in effect, made more *Other* than philosophy may describe. In both Buber and Levinas, otherness remains structured within a language that is intrinsically theological. It does so as a kind of religious defence of the ethics defended elsewhere, which one commentator refers to as Levinas' own 'mission to the gentiles'.[9] That is, a particularly Jewish framework from which a secular ethics is appropriated and explained. That framework, according to Levinas, is characterized not in terms of formulations and categories, but of a lived faith in the expediencies occurring in everyday life. It is a Judaism that becomes universal not by grand gestures or plans, but by the loving rehabilitation of a biblical application of care and responsibility. In this way, Levinas leaves behind the Greek tradition and exacts a 'moral grammar' in the 'banal acts of civility, hospitality, kindness and politeness'.[10] Again and again, this emphasis upon concrete human existence is repeated and reformulated in quasi-phenomenological language; the advent of an objective content in the human person 'outside the subject', in which God's word coincides with the nakedness of a human face and elects the self to be awoken, and to resolutely pursue the 'ethical intrigue' which comes before all knowledge.[11]

Let us return to Levinas' essay, *On the Jewish Reading of Scriptures*, in which he comments on Talmudic passages to show possible 'ways of reading' from an explicitly Jewish perspective.[12] Specifically, he pursues a plurality of hermeneutical approaches that together constitute a possible, 'path towards transcendence'.[13] The reflection upon the means of interpreting sacred texts within his own Jewish tradition is at the heart of Levinas' conceptualization of the meaning and significance of Israel. For Levinas, the sacred texts which belong to the historical community of Israel have a universal significance because they are to be interpreted in the light of contemporary problems. In the example he cites, that of commentary on the judicial punishments of Deuteronomy 25:2-3 in the Tractate Makkoth in the Babylonian Talmud, the exegesis seems to be acutely disengaged from a modern liberal perspective. The Deuteronomic references to the penalty of flogging as a possible atonement for being cut off from one's people share religious and cultural assumptions utterly foreign to a liberal mindset that avoids theological presupposition. As Levinas observes, the evocation of violent 'blows' as a just reward for a dramatic transgression that includes such guilt may 'wound our liberal souls'.[14] Not only does the punishment seem abhorrent, but also the theology it assumes appears foreign and unexplainable. As Levinas also sees clearly, the text itself, even before its historical exegesis, implies transcendence and a directionality that is inherently theological. Specifically, the notion of being cut off from the community of faith and order established by divine decree is not simply social exclusion, but also an eschatological exclusion. The one who has sinned to such a degree that he or she is cut from the community is also cut off from the future hope of salvation; and in this way, the Messianic hope of Israel is removed from the horizon of the individual. To lose one's place among God's people is to lose one's place before God. Levinas acknowledges this and nevertheless argues for the text to be taken seriously by modern readers. Despite the 'antiquated' language, Levinas argues that the various conventions assumed in the text must be accepted for the sake of understanding its content.[15]

By insisting on an intellectual hospitality for an ancient text, Levinas holds together both the importance of the concrete and localized aspects of a given text and the manner in which the world envisaged in that text clarifies the thought and the world in which the text is read today. Through a contemporary reading, a genuine meeting of one world (the present) with another world (the biblical world) occurs. The narrative form in which the meeting takes place is not ethereal, floating somewhere between the mind of the reader and the ancient world in which the original writer produced the text, but follows the form of the words themselves. One reads the text and spends some time in its world. The illumination that Levinas describes is revealed in the exegesis from the immobilized thought that arrives in the letters upon the page.[16] That is to say, the written word makes available a meaning to the reader via its exegesis, which is forever tied to the strict words and language retained on the page.

In itself, this could be argued for exegesis across various traditions. Yet for Levinas, the Jewish (and the Talmudic) tradition proffers a means of interpreting the text that is unique. The textual cadences of the Hebrew Scriptures sound forth not simply the localized moments of historical Israel, but also continue to echo in the community of Israel today. They belong not to a historical moment or epoch, but to a historical community, whose conception of God and justice remains remarkably poignant. In the pages of Deuteronomy, and in the Babylonian Talmud, Levinas finds the written witness of a living people who envision a God whose justice outweighs the power of evil. Specifically, the cutting off from one's own people is an example of the crucial dimension of community to the life of faith. Despite the tragic results of being cut off – loss of family, friendship and access to basic necessities, and equally the isolated exposure to the elements and violent enemies – Levinas notes that the human tribunal has the responsibility to dispense mercy and justice, and to find a way to overcome the original sin that provoked such terrible punishment. While flogging is an excessive violence in its own way, it is offered as a means to expiate the punished from the necessity of being driven out into the wilderness. And furthermore, the flogging is limited to 40 stripes (Deut 25:3), to show that justice is tempered by mercy. Levinas highlights the word 'brother' in this text, which indicates the fraternity of the human community despite the seriousness of sin. Fraternity, for Levinas, proceeds from a responsibility for other persons and indicates that any punishment meted out to the sinner must be devoid of the 'spirit of violence, contempt or hatred'.[17] If the community is built on an authentic fraternity, the divine laws stand over a web of relationships that are oriented towards justice and mercy, rather than injustice and hatred. The punishment is hard because the sin against God and community carries an eternal consequence. Its basis in the divine laws is not the content of the laws as such, but divine paternity, which rests not upon the human community but upon God's self-revelation. For the community to look upon God as a paternal point of reference is for the community also to look upon itself as a fraternal society bound together under a common and indisputable judgement. What may be called human mercy is not given priority over the strict adherence to a divine law given for the benefit of the community of the faithful.

In this way, the Jewish conception of the community of faith appears largely juridical; it seems lacking in the qualities of mercy and compassion. But this is precisely what Levinas wishes to overcome. He does so by reference to Exodus 34:7:

[The Lord keeps] steadfast love for thousands [of generations], forgiving iniquity and transgression and sin, but who will by no means clear the guilty, visiting the iniquity of the fathers upon the children and the children's children, to the third and the fourth generation . . .

Here, Levinas notes the vast difference between the longevity of God's 'steadfast love' and his return of 'iniquity' upon the descendants of the guilty. In the former, God's love remains constant for thousands of generations (and for subsequent Rabbis, this is interpreted for at least 2000 years). In the latter, those guilty of grave sin will have their iniquity lavished upon their descendants for only four generations. As Levinas notes, compassion is 'thus five hundred times greater than divine severity'.[18] Moreover, the gratuitousness of divine compassion is the rewarding counterpart to the divine restriction of life's baser tendencies. The restrictive interdicts appear as negative experiences of human life, whereas they can only be interpreted alongside the reward of compassion or mercy. Levinas sees clearly that the power of constraint is not in itself a negative provocation deflecting human experience from that which is desired, but a positive provocation towards the good. Thus, the constraints of Leviticus 18, in which sexual interdicts are privileged examples, are a divine affirmation of the rewards that come from restraining a search for the 'blind abundance' of sexual desire.[19] For Levinas, any preference for a life lived solely within the ambience of its own self-generating desire; of wild, animal vitality and the intoxication of one's own essence, is a circuitous route within one's uniquely limited circumference. The limitations of the Law hold one back from this self-referential orientation, not simply through specific moral acts, but via an authentic openness to otherness. Such openness interrupts the radar of one's self-reference and invites the self outside circular habits of despairing self-intoxication.

The vast distance between God's compassion and the visitation of iniquity upon the guilty is an important point of reference in this account of Israel's law. Levinas sees in the Jewish account of the Law that sits under divine paternity an enactment of true community (Israel) and the opening up of the human person to authenticity. The fraternity of Israel rests upon this familial proportionality between God the Father and God's people as his children. Glory appears in those acts of abeyance to the Law that upholds the healthy distinction between God and the people. And this is the point at which Levinas turns to an imminent account of the compassion that lasts thousands of generations. While God's compassion is said to transcend the limitations of time and generational change, it cannot be known in anything except the pressing exigencies of the present self-sacrificial moment. Levinas notes the necessity in Scripture that one person take responsibility for another. In the case he discusses from Deuteronomy, the judges themselves take responsibility for the one who has sinned and been punished with being cut off from the community. The justice rendered to the guilty party is not human but divine justice, and there must always be those whose office obliges them to take on the responsibility of a moral judgement concerning the accused. Because this responsibility is of such a high quality – 'whereby one person assumes the destiny and the very existence of another' – it falls outside freedom as it is normally understood.[20] The judge, or indeed any who takes on such a complete responsibility, is acting out of an obligation which is fundamental not only to the Law, but also to the success of authentic human community, and therefore to an 'ontological structure' that precedes freedom.[21] In this way, responsibility belongs to that which, as Levinas argues, is anterior to freedom and which defines the meaning of the term 'God'.[22] The compassion of God, which is opened up by the self-restraint of the negative commands within each human life, is given as a possibility within the truly ethical moment of self-giving for the sake of another. This cannot be understood apart from the gulf between compassion and punishment and the divine enactment of mercy in the face of hatred.

It can be seen that for Levinas, the Jewish conception of God is derived from a reading of the Scriptures within a community that honours justice and mercy. In particular, it is a community that views in the ethical moment the content of God's own compassion, which lasts for thousands of years. The very endurance of divine compassion stands as a dramatic affront to the power of evil, which in any case is itself a return of itself upon itself. Recall the words of Exodus, '. . . visiting the inequity of the fathers upon the children and the children's children . . .' God's compassion derives from Himself, but the punishment of the wicked derives from their own negative actions. Levinas' philosophy intersects profoundly here with his exegesis. The human response to alterity is fundamental to his account of the Jewish reading of Scriptures, and the relationship between ethics and theology is noticeable. The ethical act is the concretization of justice one-for-another. It is

necessarily self-sacrificial. Furthermore, authentic religion is, for
Levinas, a transcendence that receives its general content from
ethics. Levinas refers approvingly to the interpretative work of
Rabbi Hananiah b. 'Akashia, for whom justice is invoked as a
kind of glory for both God and the tribunal and judges of the
world. This glory is one in which justice is rendered in the
world and from which religious transcendence manifests itself.
As Levinas argues:

> In the justice of the Rabbis, difference retains its
> meaning. Ethics is not simply the corollary of the
> religious but is, itself, the element in which religious
> transcendence receives its original meaning.

This is the radical thought that arises in Levinas' other works,
and notably in both *Totality and Infinity* and *Otherwise than Being*,
that ethics is a form of religious transcendence in its first and
most significant degree. Yet here it is not a phenomenological
disclosure, but the way in which Levinas reads the rabbinical
tradition. It is the notion that the thought of God rises in
the authentic ethical act of self-deprecation before the other
person. In this way, religious transcendence offers a content
that is received from the agency of one person acting ethically
in the space of difference before the other person.

Now, the Levinasian turn towards the concrete face-to-
face moment does not eradicate the need for exegesis. On the
contrary, the destiny of Israel is not simply to construct an
authentically ethical community, but also to study and interpret
the biblical texts. For Levinas, it is helpful to understand the
community of Israel as a plurality of people caught up in a
moment of the signification of meaning.[23] Meaning, largely,
is derived from the Scriptures. In the midst of such a people,
known as the people of the Book, there is constant recollection
of sacred texts and their study in the form of continual
liturgical activity. The multiple meanings and the complexity of
significations which derive from studious attention to Scripture

in the context of prayer are illustrative of Levinas' account of the role of Israel. For him, this is an inspired community for which the familial relationship between God and the people presupposes a robust account of compassion. The occurrence of the encounter between the text and the people is an important orientation in human subjectivity towards authentic alterity. It is so because it is a proximity between the human self and alterity as a concrete presence that provokes an experience of the glory of which Levinas notes in keeping the Law. This glory is not of a perfect transcendence, but of a localized encounter with the Other. For this reason, Levinas refers to the faith of Israel as a 'simple faith'.[24] It is the enactment of faith in the form of a sensitive commitment to that which is authentic. In a sense, the encounter with the text and then conversely with other persons who act as ambassadors of need and responsibility is such that it is a faith stripped down to its bare humility and a simplicity that cannot hold firm to every exegetical conclusion. It cannot hold every answer and is unable to experience the perspective of every person. By becoming aware of this truth, it acts humbly and simply in respecting the differences of the Rabbis and the scholars, clinging carefully to a responsibility for that which it has received. This includes the text, its exegesis (even in plurality) and other persons.

Here again, Levinas coincides the ethical proximity that he finds in Scripture with the notion of 'awakening'.[25] To find oneself before the height of another is itself *ethics* as Levinas understands it. It is the ethical moment *par excellence*, in which truth is revealed as a quality of responsibility in the face of a great height. As such, it is an intimacy in relation to that which is both proximate and transcendent, and which awakens a listening heart within the non-reciprocal relationship with the Other. And to what precisely is one awakened to? Following his account of the Jewish reading of God and compassion, Levinas answers, 'the face of the other man'.[26] In this subtle, almost derivative moment of life's typical events and experiences, God's presence coincides with the unique form of the face of the

Other. The face-to-face, for Levinas, is not only a transcendent moment, but is itself transcendence. In being awakened (not simply woken up, but, as it were, provoked to desire upwards towards the Other) in this proximity, one is aware that one is not experiencing a spatial or cosmological height. This is not the other person standing over the oneself in temporality and nor is it a mystical appeal to the stars above as one ponders other people. No, the light that shines down upon the self is an incarnate presence of the other person that calls forth from an ethical signification experienced as a transcendence in relation to one's own self. To be awakened towards the Other, one must assumedly be orientated already away from the Other. Levinas thinks of each person as, essentially, consigned to the bedding of 'preformed and customary ideas that protect and reassure'.[27] The awakening that Levinas believes occurs in ethical proximity is evidenced in the simplicity of Jewish faith, by which the sacred literature of the tradition makes apparent the otherness of other persons. That is, the faithful read the Scriptures and God's justice invokes in them an awareness of ethical proximity. The biblical assurance of God's compassion overcomes the intransigent obstacles that are placed between the self and the need evident in the faces of other people. The form of the Bible; its immediate lessons, characters and narratives, still holds the dogmatic content of God in the forefront of meaning for the reader. But they also provoke an affective sense of the call of the other person, thus 'forcing us out' of bed, to continue Levinas' metaphor.[28] Such an awakening breaks the self out of its self-recurring thematic of sameness and muted awareness of others.

Levinas speaks of a 'little faith', the term from which the title of the present chapter takes its name.[29] He sees in this description not a belittling term but a positive embrace of faith's necessary humility before God and others. For him, the Scriptures are a means by which alterity is broken open to the simple believer and so humble awareness of one's limited vocation is a help. But there is something further in that Levinas, in the final passages of his essay, takes hold of the interpretative approach to Scripture that privileges a simple reading of sacred texts. He indicates the need to avoid a speculative or philological reading of the texts, even if this means living with the more difficult ambiguities suggested in the form of transcendence that biblical texts convey. He writes:

> Let us prefer, then, the genesis of every text to its exegesis, the certainties of given signs to the hazards of mysterious messages, the combinations of the shadows in the Cave to the uncertain calls from outside! This is also a science, at times an admirable one, to destroy false prophecies.[30]

Hence, this chapter refers to Levinas' preference for the shadows. He appeals for the enactment of Israel's simple faith in the observance of the Law and in the keeping of Scriptures. Of course, Levinas upholds the necessity for interpretation, but lays greater stress on an exegesis that acknowledges an authentic meeting with alterity; with God through the proximity of the other person. It avoids the seeming glory of truths fully known, and, countering Plato's famous cave metaphor, encourages thinkers to explore the ambiguous shadows on the cave walls rather than think themselves capable of a comprehensive knowledge outside. The hermeneutic that is more fundamental for Levinas' account of Israel's faith is not the scholar's exegetical task, but the logic that follows a close reading of the texts. For Levinas, that logic is the concretization of ethics as responsibility for the Other. Indeed, the reading of the text itself is a responsible activity that requires a self-effacing quality in the reader. As the above quote makes clear, Levinas privileges the genesis of the text to its exegesis, highlighting the concrete form of the text over the development of exegetical study. Equally, he is suspicious of the mystical tendencies in other readings of Scripture, rebuking the 'hazards of mysterious messages' in favour of the 'certainties of given signs'.[31] Biblical references within the framework of their own religious assumptions and narrative dimensions are, in Levinas' terms, more reliable for their tendency towards clarity and the observance of richly textured content than for the seeking out of mystery for its own sake.

One can also find here a hint of suspicion in relation to overtly prophetic readings of Scripture. Levinas does not reject prophecy *per se*; rather he endorses it on the grounds that it does not seek to be prophetic. In other words, the true prophet does not wish to prophecy, but to tell the truth. Authentic prophecy seeks out truth and its proclamation; it does not stir up others for the sake of a rebellious disposition. In fact, the truly prophetic is not the public display of the personal subject, but the faithful turn to holy texts and a desire to enact their lessons well. Levinas appeals to the Platonic image of the Cave to affirm the shadows of Scripture over against the calls from outside. He does not unpack this image, but it is clear that the mysterious elements of Scripture, or those passages in which no absolute interpretation can be made, or texts from which a seemingly endless multitude of meaning has been drawn for generations, are a preferred combination of truths in half-light than those texts or words which derive from outside. Levinas does not reject the latter, but prefers the former. As such, the half-light of Scripture is preferable to the full spectacle of the visible world outside. This is more than rhetoric. Levinas makes a remarkably conservative hermeneutical statement for the sake of a radical end. He is holding fast to the text on the basis of its role in the community of faith. Furthermore, he appeals for a preference for the simpler textual forms of sacred Scripture over non-Scriptural texts. This is not a form of fideism. Levinas does not reject other disciplines or sources of knowledge. Instead, his strict observance of the texts in themselves holds together the radical dismantling of evil and injustice with the event or the thought of God. By remaining close to such texts – preferring their shadows to the words of others – he makes available a counter-cultural moment of religious transcendence in an act of faith. It is counter-cultural in the sense that the strict observance of the text and its opening up to the other constitutes the fundamental commitment; other commitments, be they economic, social, familial and so forth, are secondary. And for Levinas, such a radical faith, which remains proximate to the Scriptures, is an authentic Jewish faith that, in turn, authenticates the face-to-face encounter with other persons. By this requisite fidelity to the texts, Levinas' ethics envisages an Israel that holds firmly to a simple faith that prefers the shadows.

Levinas' simple faith seems at home in the most quotidian aspects of human experience. Because his depiction of a textual faith is suspicious of either gnosis or mysticism, it must avoid intentional displays of religion, at least in day-to-day life. That is not to say it usurps religious practices, but rather that religion itself is to coincide with the recurrence of activities and inter-subjective encounters that, on the face of it, appear bereft of intentional religious character. As it is shown elsewhere, the very thought of God returns in the ethical moment. Despite this, it must be repeated that the claim of a faith that remains intensely close to the texts themselves remains at odds with a culture that is itself suspicious of dogma or religious conviction that spills over the boundaries of occasional festivals and private devotional practices. If the community to which Levinas refers, that of Israel, is indeed a historical community in which faith plays a central role, it must be asked what Levinas means by such a group.

In the post-World War II publication of essays, *Difficult Freedom*, Levinas ponders on the significance of the Jewish people. His thought bears a strong European focus amidst reflections on the historical development of Jewish religious culture and practice. And moreover, Levinas emphasizes once more the crucial role of the sacred texts as the centrepiece of Jewish faith. For example, he upholds the State of Israel as a moment of authentic achievement, but only insofar as it retains its connection with Jewish religion in the form of rabbinical exegesis. The Bible remains at the heart of Judaism, even in this modern statist example. He writes, '[t]his exegesis made the text speak; while critical philology speaks *of* this text'.[32] Levinas strongly contrasts rabbinical exegesis, which occurs within a tradition of religious observance that spans history, with modern critical methods that are not exegesis as such, but rather philology.

The radical nature of Levinas' description of the relationship between the Jews and the Scriptures consists in the orientation of the reader to the text. For Levinas, the text must be liberated to speak directly to those who struggle through their exegesis, and so a reader is not oriented simply towards the written page, but allows himself or herself to be redirected by the text. This is a rebuke to modern methods of interpretation. For Levinas, this presupposes the existence of a historical community whose manifestation in a modern political form such as the State of Israel is legitimated not by modernity, but by the holy words of previous generations. For Levinas, '[t]he Jewish people therefore achieves a State whose prestige none the less stems from the religion which modern political life supplants'.[33] Levinas, therefore, makes a strong defence for the religious – and therefore theological – basis for the State of Israel.

So, a modern conceptualization of the Jewish people is intimately connected with the existence of the State of Israel. For Levinas, this is a modern State that is not founded on a typical modern basis. It relies on sacred texts and the interpretative community of the Jews as a people who share a covenantal view of their association with God and the world. As the above has argued, a hermeneutical preference is made for the ambiguities of the Scriptures – preferring the *shadows* – than for the certainties of foreign ideas. The religious foundations of Israel in the modern world are, therefore, inseparable from their political machinations.

One can see immediately how problematic this might become. To link a theological mooring to the expression of a statist form of governance, and to imply a religious association, however tenuous, between its policy and its Scriptures, is to tempt fate. That is to say, the State of Israel may pursue policies that are inimical to the very Scriptures that legitimate its basic institutional structures in the first place. One does not need to document the formal conflicts between Palestinians and Israel to show that such an association is a dangerous move. Levinas offers an answer to this danger that is only partially convincing. For him, the basis for Israel's existence is only an aspect of the story and what is necessary is to describe its vocation in the modern world. In Levinas' words, that vocation is to offer the opportunity to finally carry out the 'social law of Judaism'.[34] For him, the social law is the enactment of authentic justice. Levinas views the existence of the State of Israel as the historical epoch in which a true justice, inspired and provoked by the Scriptures, may be concretized in history. That, for him, is the high vocation of the Jewish people and it is the form of true religion. Authentic religion is the carrying out of the Law, and by this it can be seen that justice is the '*raison d'être* of the State: that is religion'.[35] Authentic religion, according to Levinas, is the enactment of the appropriate course of ethical action in the space between persons. It is the hovering ethical proximity of a call to justice that is absolute. Such a religion is not easily recognized, and may well remain always an invisible truth of existence. Evidence for its authenticity lies in the fact of external religious commitment shown by the Jewish people, even in the face of historical antagonism. In this, Levinas offers the religious habits and rituals of his Jewish faith as an ethical resistance to modernity. He sees in Judaism a 'non-coincidence with its time, within coincidence', an anachronistic radicalism that refuses the modernist desire to conform to one's time and to renounce interiority and truth.[36] Judaism, where it is a commitment to the order of authentic encounters with its own living texts, remains a prophetic witness to an eternity deeper than time, and one whose commitment to justice bulwarks against the false messianisms of the present or any other age. The true religion of Judaism resists both the incursions and the hesitations of false religion and ideology, because its engagement with Scripture is a face-to-face encounter with texts from a time that surpasses the limitations of time. The Jewish liturgical tradition upholds the continued reading and study of the sacred texts, and with eyes open can embrace those in need of justice while prophetically warning against the false eternities of human constructs not bound to either texts or authentic persons.[37] This resistant dimension provides a partial defence of Levinas' position on the State of Israel, but cannot answer in full the problematic nature of a theological basis for Israel's modern political institutional forms.

Of course, this is a remarkably positive account of Judaism's ability both to resist and to overcome the limitations of the modern world. Not only does it view the religious foundations of the modern State of Israel as integral, but also does it view this model as an authentic expression of the Jewish vocation more generally. Furthermore, it is a vocation universalized in that it belongs to each individual Jewish person, regardless of formal national allegiance. Elsewhere, Levinas personalizes his response to the universal vocation of Israel in these words: 'To "go up" into Israel for a French Jew is certainly not to change nationality, it is to respond to a vocation'.[38] There is a co-alliance of the vocation of Israel with the movement of the Jewish person (and in Levinas' case, that of the French citizen). And in terms of its descriptions of vocation, it illustrates the significance of a people whose communal convictions are inspired by the notion of divine revelation in the pages of their sacred works. A people who maintain a rigorous adherence to commands that are utterly bewildering to a modern sensibility is not only eccentric, but also testament to authentic human experience unencumbered by the limitations of modernity. They give witness to an account of justice that avoids entrenched ideological or political commitments and honours the extant moment of need in other persons. They do this without departure from the model of Israel that Levinas endorses and consequently with an abiding historical relationship with both the virtues and the sins of that model. The virtues of the model lie in a concrete religious resistance to modernity in its most totalitarian tendencies. Unfortunately, the sins of that model betray a willingness to supersede the religious resistance to totalitarianism and resort to the worst banalities of modern state violence and politics.

For the above reasons, Levinas' account of the State of Israel is controversial and not entirely convincing. In an article in the journal *Esprit*, he declared that Zionist hopes constituted a dream that began in implausible nostalgia, reaching back to the very sources of Creation, echoing forth their highest expectations.[39] The notion that a divine mandate sits at the basis for Israel's political claims cannot be ruled out from Levinas' language. Again, the religious dimension of the Jewish people cannot be severed from its political manifestation in a modern state and Levinas explicitly defends this; certainly, he refers to the 'profane forms' assumed by the State, but still insists that the State of Israel cannot be separated from its religious origins.[40] In two other essays, he explores the question of Zionism further, *The State of Caesar and the State of David*, and *Politics After!* In both, Zionism is a political fact encountered in the historical interplay of Jewish faith, Scripture and the politics of the twentieth century. In the latter, he speaks of Israel's 'difficult freedom', which is the troubling event of an 'extreme form of human potential'.[41] This potential is for an ethical future in which justice might be the normative practice of the State of Israel. In this sense, it is a spiritual ambition, for it must be remembered that for Levinas, ethics and authentic religion coincide. Yet it is this laboured emphasis upon the ethical potential of the State of Israel that concedes what is most unconvincing in Levinas' account of the vocation of the Jewish people. Levinas so intertwines the vocation of the Jews with the State of Israel that the ethical purchase of both is placed in the grip of a potential future tense. Levinas speaks of the vocation of the State of Israel as the manifestation of justice. Yet he accentuates the notion that the modern State, founded on the land promised to the heirs of Abraham, is the opportunity for a 'political doctrine suitable for monotheists'.[42] For him, the modern structures of the State of Israel both coincide with the kinds of statist structures evident in other nations and differ from them by virtue of their intrinsic relationship with the sacred Scriptures of Judaism. In particular, the Torah is not of historical interest only, but is also a living textual basis for the State's existence. In terms of its contemporary vocation, Levinas cannot point to the enactment of justice as a historical reality, nor to ethics as a concretized practice in the substantive events of the Israeli populace from one day to the next. Instead, he must offer a messianic hope for such things to be developed in an open future. Perhaps this is Levinas' expression of a political faith, or of an ethical eschatology. In any case, time and experience are not friends to this theory. After all, the State of Israel was established in 1948 and decades later Levinas can only say: 'But all has just begun'.[43]

In this optimistic sense of what might be hoped for in contemporary Judaism, Levinas' conception of Israel's vocation can be witnessed. Because it is a hope that relies on a theological basis – that of the sacred texts at the foundations – it cannot be restricted to philosophical categories. The hope that Levinas conveys is linked to the transcendence to which the Scriptures witness in the concrete political problems of the present moment. In itself, the theologian can detect a positive association of the testament of the texts and the fellowship of a historical community of faith. It cannot be assumed to be a robust ecclesiology, but it certainly gives the sense of a Jewish approach to contemporary engagement with Scripture that honours the localized and culturally specific referents in Biblical literature with the pressing needs of the world as they are experienced. These are sentiments that resonate with the hope that the community of the faithful might be an authentic *communio* of difference, united by a common faith. It is also the case that Levinas' reading of the Scriptures from within the historical community of the Jewish faith, albeit within a

Talmudic framework, offers a point of convergence with Christian theology. Yet, Levinas hopes for too much from the State of Israel.

This helps explain why, in an essay on the relationship between Christianity and Judaism, Levinas notes his own changing attitude.[44] He acknowledges that his Lithuanian childhood afforded little engagement with Christianity, and that the horrors of the Spanish Inquisition and the Crusades loomed darkly over his perception of Christian history. Then he came to read the Gospel and see in it the 'representation and the teaching of what is human'.[45] His direct experience of a central Christian text (and especially the words of Matt 25) shone new light on the Christian narrative, revealing a theology of God in which the suffering Other – the widow, the poor, the orphan – was associated with the person of the persecuted God. Levinas saw in Matthew's Gospel a shared sense of the teaching in Isaiah 58, in which God is found in the suffering servant and in those who are underfoot or persecuted. While the clear teaching of both Old and New Testaments on the priority given to the poor is acceptable to him, Levinas notes his own incomprehension at the dogmatic content of Christianity, of the realist theology surrounding Christ. In connection with this, he cannot accept the concept of transubstantiation in the Eucharist, for to him this bypasses the substance of alterity given in the face of the other person. He writes:

> . . . I would tell myself that the true communion was
> in the meeting with the other, rather than in the bread
> and the wine, and that it was in that encounter that the
> personal presence of God resided . . .[46]

Here, Levinas views one particular doctrine of Catholic Christianity as antithetical to his notion of human alterity. For him, the Eucharist is not a meeting of disciples with the person of Christ as such, but an unnecessary dogmatic avoidance of authentic otherness. There is no doubt that he misses a fundamental feature of the Eucharist, that it remains a communal event in which Christians, side by side, receive a particular presence in a certain passivity. The Christian person stands in the Eucharistic assembly in a radical displacement of all external titles, hierarchical dispositions and roles. Each man and woman receives the consecrated elements in a spirit of common partnership before the divine mercy, and so the alterity experienced in that communal order is one that resides in humility before otherness. While Levinas can recognize other Christian concepts such as God's kenosis, divine humility and so forth, as sharing a Jewish sensibility, he cannot forge the link between these and the event of Christian liturgy in the specifically Christian context.

Moreover, Levinas points towards a historical reality that Christians will find disheartening. He sees in the sign of the Christ (the cross), a symbol that has been linked frightfully to incomprehensible moments of evil. Certain acts (one assumes he thinks of the Inquisition and Crusades as above) were undertaken despite the Christian patrimony instilled in their perpetrators. This becomes more precise in considering the Holocaust, in which Catholics and Protestants participated without considering any interdiction posed in the baptism they received as children.[47] This is of course a terrible epoch of European history, and indeed Levinas views Christianity as ultimately unable to withstand Europe's historical march towards its most diabolical temptations. There are of course a great number of murderous regimes that have rippled across the face of the globe, but the Holocaust stands as a particularly European moment that carries a certain power over the collective imagination. Any person of faith, Christian or otherwise, who has taken the opportunity to visit Auschwitz and to walk among the tilted bed frames, or into the hollowed gas chambers, or on the long troughs provided as shared lavatories, will discover a certain shortness of breath at the veracity of it all. Europe, whose history is so intertwined with the Christian faith, could not stop itself from this, and allowed such a high degree of bureaucratic efficiency in the rendering of the Shoah, that it ought to challenge the conceptualization of faith and culture. This is why Levinas finds it difficult to reconcile the good he recognizes in Christian texts with the evidence of history. Furthermore, Levinas' personal experiences are a conflicted narrative of positive and negative experiences of Christians and their faith. For example, his wife and daughter were spared their lives through the ministry of cloistered nuns and the friendship of Catholics. Levinas respected the substance of the Gospel, but thought it forever compromised by history.[48] For him, the encounter with Christianity is a contrast of his 'little faith' with something otherwise. Despite this, in particular moments of encounter he found that Judaism and Christianity met in a shared spiritual space. He recounts the story of a funeral service in May 1940, in which he recognized the figure of Hannah leading her son Samuel to the Temple, in a painting upon the church wall.[49] Hannah, the one who poured out her soul to the Lord (1 Samuel), was a kind of kenosis that Levinas viewed as authentic and concrete.

The authenticity of both Christianity and Judaism is a central theme for Franz Rosenzweig, in whom Levinas sees a prophetic voice. Rosenzweig almost became a Christian, but turned to the faith of his ancestors in an evangelical moment of conversion. His great work, *The Star of Redemption*, constitutes a strange coincidence of the mystical and the philosophical in its rendering of Christianity and Judaism as living embodiments of authentic truths.[50] Levinas interprets the great Jewish philosopher as marking out metaphysical truth along two paths (Jewish and Christian), thus concentrating truth fundamentally as a positive plurality in the world. It is not that truth itself is divided, but rather that truth has a merciful capacity for multiple expressions that are non-contradictory, and so 'dialogue' and 'symbiosis' are made possible.[51] In both, Levinas does not mean occasions of dialogue, but literally the sustained closeness of being which in science refers to two species living and interacting. The evolution and mutual development of Judaism and Christianity requires an attentiveness one to another, and a constancy of spirit for their shared success. Levinas pursues this within a creatively critical orientation towards Christianity and does not hesitate to remind its protagonists that during the Crusades, Christ did not step down from the symbol of the cross to halt their behaviour.[52] Christians are called to account for the sins of their predecessors, or at least for those done in Christ's name and under the symbol of his cross. For Levinas, history stands in judgement upon Christians, but not upon their central texts. In his reading of the Gospel, of the good news that sits at the heart of Christian theology, he finds a direct affirmation of God in the person of Christ and in the poor and the suffering. Furthermore, despite his accent upon historical abuses, Levinas contends a mutual authentication in the meeting of Judaism and Christianity through a strong reorientation towards their Scriptures. This would be true to Rosenzweig's understanding of the two metaphysical paths, as well as Levinas' philosophy. To recall Levinas' notion of the ethical content of alterity, he views not in the meeting with another person a proportional mutuality, but of an 'exigency that increases as one responds to it', and to a glory of the infinite in the appearance of 'Other' who 'disturbs or tears out of his repose'.[53] The other – Levinas' *Other* – is one who disturbs the self and awakens it to an infinite ethical responsibility. In Levinas' interviews and Jewish commentaries, he harnesses the insights of a lived historical Judaism to engage with the otherness of Christianity in just such a way as this. Yet he insists: it remains a mutual responsibility, and Christian theology, therefore, must remain acutely interested in Jewish faith and practice, and always anchored within the orbit of its own central texts.

Within this mutualizing authenticity, Levinas does not forget the peculiar vocation of the Jewish people in its 'little faith'. In his eyes, theirs is a vocation that shows the way of justice to Europe and to the world. In Michael Morgan's account of Levinas' thought, a key role is to demonstrate the ethical character of European and Western society.[54] The notion of justice as a demonstration before others ensures a strong connection between the Jews as a people with a vocation, and with the contextual topography in which they act; in other words, the world. Justice is not only to be done and seen, but also to be felt and experienced. This is not a bare spiritualism, with no awareness of the complexities and surfaces of concrete sociality. On the contrary, the vocation of the Jews constitutes, in Morgan's words, an 'austere humanism', which has been touched deeply by the events of the Holocaust.[55] It carries the same degree of responsibility Levinas identifies in his philosophical analysis of alterity. In other words, a responsibility that is always excessive. It tends towards an activity that stands outside the precarious inefficacy of human action by reaching higher, forgetting its limitations and acting for the other person in an authenticating ethics of care and response.[56] The very universality of such an ethics is concretized in the disinterested responsibility of the concrete moment before the particular other. As the Jew bears up within this arc of responsibility, he or she is a manifestation of the responsibility evinced in the sacred works of the tradition. More generally, the Jewish community bears the truth of God taught in the Scriptures, which is antithetical to the concepts of God wrought in the modern Western philosophical stable. The God of Abraham, Isaac and Jacob is not a God of concepts or categories, for if this were so then God would be a tamed concept Himself, situated in 'being's move'.[57] Because of this attestation to the God of the Scriptures, Levinas argues that the activity of justice derives from the idea of God presented in those texts, which stands outside Being as such. In fact, the Jewish faith presents to Europe and the world a means of rescuing Greek categories of Being – and ontology more generally – from their own self-contained captivity, because it offers a radically infinite God who is not bound to philosophy. Levinas does not call for the Jewish conceptualization to displace that of Greek philosophy, but to correct it. Here, Levinas takes up Descartes' idea of God as a *cogito* which to begin with contains the *cogitation*, and in turn signifies that which is non-contained and non-containable.[58] For Descartes, the infinity that the notion of God contains is an idea so perfectly outside human experience, that its origins could not be said to have been derived within the human mind.[59] The Jews, as a people, bear this testimony by virtue of their texts and tradition, and this vocation is an ethical gift to the world.

Nevertheless, Levinas does not construct a theology of God that issues the latter as numinous in any way. In an essay written at the same time he was completing *Totality and Infinity*, he calls for a 'religion for adults', in which infantile constructs of God are set aside.[60] Levinas refers strikingly to the Holocaust, arguing that unique among the millions who suffered, the Jews knew a complete dereliction; the intent of destructing their entire race marked them out in all the world. He makes the startling observation that the Holocaust returned the Jews to the centre of world religious consciousness and re-establishes the link between present-day Israel and the Israel of the Bible.[61] In this historical breaking apart of the Jewish narrative, their self-identification with those who had been in Egypt is assured, and also for Levinas, the Jewish rejection of the numinous or the sacred, as some religious traditions would define those terms. Levinas insists that the Jewish faith protects the absolute freedom of the human person, denying all spiritual feelings of surpluses, sacramentality or indeed any experience that envelops and transports the self away.[62] Once again, the austere humanism that Morgan refers to above shows itself in Levinas as an ethical foil to any hint of mysticism or spiritual rapture. It is a humanism that is constantly driven towards its own sacred texts, and in turn encounters the thought of God as a denial of idolatry and superstition, rebuking false spiritualisms and prayerful flights of ecstasy. In Levinas' reading of his own tradition, the community of faith appeals to the wisdom of God in the human condition, to the intelligence of reasoned thought that permeates the Jewish religion in its moments of glory. By doing this, the Jews protect the action of free being, and so open up divinity from the encounter with the other human person in the liberating bounds of an austere humanism that is not subject to politics, ideology or government. In this way, it is an-archic. It refuses every outside imposition and seeks to honour the good, over and against all intervention. It is both universal and always engaged in the particular. As Adriaan Peperzak puts it:

> Israel's universality, however, is the essential feature of its particularity; its essence consists in its being the servant of the whole universe for an ethical service beyond politics.[63]

The 'beyond politics' is the ethical responsibility that envelopes the self on behalf of the other person. In this way, the Jewish vocation is both linked to its theology of God and being entirely displaced by it. On the one hand, it derives precisely from the God of justice who speaks to the particular people of faith in the Scriptures. On the other, its very reliance on the Scriptural testimony of God places the Jewish people not at the service of themselves and their theology, but at the service of others. In other words, the theology that Levinas reads in the Scriptures dislocates his people from these moorings, in effect releasing them to move outwards in orientation to the suffering Other. And in any case, once unmoored (in an ethical and not in an historical or strictly theological sense) to act well for others, the Jew finds divinity once again in the context of the human. This, for Levinas, is what it is for the Jew to embrace a religion for adults. There, before the face of the other person, Levinas locates the coalface of the Jewish vocation, which is an election of utter humility and responsibility:

> This election is made up not of privileges but of responsibilities. It is a nobility based not on royalties [droit d'auteur] or a birthright [droit d'aînesse] conferred by a divine caprice, but on the position of each human I [moi].[64]

The election of the Jew, and the whole people of Israel, is a calling out of the self towards the Other. It is not the conferral of titles or categories of esteem, but of a holy deprivation before the alterity that shines in the face and faces of others. God alights in this moment, and is witnessed in the activity of justice. Elsewhere, Levinas refers to a supreme 'quietude' that defines Judaism.[65] That is, a restless silence that takes in eternity itself, even as its eyes are fixed firmly upon the suffering Other in the present moment. In this sense, Judaism steps into the light of an ethical moment which summons all of humanity. The same level of ethical responsibility is demanded by all, but must first be given in the realm of the particular, that it might be applied in the infinite moments of the universal. Indeed, the light is cast first on Israel, that it might infract among every people.[66]

The Levinasian embrace of the people of Israel as a historical community with a particular vocation is difficult to categorize in relation to his philosophy. As was discussed above, he emphasizes the text to a remarkable degree, and there is no doubt that his philosophical emphasis upon alterity and ethical proximity intersect profoundly with his Talmudic lectures and comments he makes on matters relating to Jewish faith. The particularism of the Jewish tradition, for Levinas, does not confound its universalism, and indeed they necessitate each other. The localized histories of Judaism are given, largely through Scripture, for the sake of all humanity, as Levinas insists.[67] It is the givenness for others that marks Israel out as the particular one-for-the-others; the people set aside by God who is the first Other, and who provokes the loving desire for the good of all other others. In fact, it is for Levinas a central Jewish tenet that an authentic community of faith is guided not by dogmatic content, let alone a *theology*, but by the self-sacrificial relationship of persons. As Richard A. Cohen puts it, Levinas' notion of religion is not the disclosure of Being, but of the transcendence that occurs in the relationship of '*beings as beings to other beings*'.[68] Cohen rightly identifies that for Levinas, an adequate expression of this is found not in ontology or theology, but in morality and justice. This helps to explain Levinas' coincidence of religion with ethics in his account of Israel's vocation. It is a vocation fundamentally disinterested by the inculcation in Western thought of ontological emphases that disenfranchise the Other. For Levinas, they include Christian theology. For Levinas' Jewish tradition, this requires a radical dislocation of theological language from positions of privilege, and a constant re-evaluation of the terms in which others are spoken of and treated.

If Levinas' account of Israel is to be concretized and drawn upon theologically, then it necessitates a constant surveillance of what he calls a 'suspect ontology'; of the preference for objective content and distinctions without regarding the suffering Other.[69] The Other, whose ethical proximity is the moment in which God's thought once again rises to awaken the self to alterity, becomes the authenticating truth in any encounter. Levinas' preference for the divine title of 'Father of orphans and defender of widows' becomes not a rallying cry, but a sober observance of a biblical and ethical truth.[70] As such, it has the capacity to characterize a theological ethics with an emphasis upon that which Levinas finds crucial in explaining Judaism: a persistence in recognizing the relationship between a living community of faith in history with its textual foundations and an attentiveness to others in their concrete suffering. As such, theology is provoked by Levinas to attend carefully to its own sacred texts and to heed their insistence on an ethics of profound concern for the divine alterity that loves without reserve. Theology learns from Levinas and his conceptualization of Judaism that a living religion achieves nothing more radical than a rigorous love for the living textures of its own demanding texts.

Chapter 6

The Return of God?

As the previous chapters described, much of Levinas' philosophy is an attempt to think and act after the horrors of the twentieth century and the Holocaust. The attempted eradication of the Jews during World War II and the same persecution of other minorities was for Levinas not simply a moral horror, but one that manifested the philosophical failure of Europe. It inspired him to approach that which is different from oneself – the Other – in ethical terms rather than by a commitment to Being as such. After the Holocaust, God-talk was viewed as problematic. How could the term 'God' have any meaning, when the Jewish people, God's chosen people, could be persecuted so brutally? In this chapter, it is shown that Levinas' attempts to think and write after the Holocaust offer the occasion of the 'return of God'. He does so from the perspective of one who suffered and lost loved ones to German National Socialism, but also one who thinks creatively from the perspective of a complex relationship between his Jewish religion and his philosophy. Always, his thought bears the imprint of the tragedy of the Holocaust. In fact, he devotes his second major work, *Otherwise Than Being or Beyond Essence*, to victims of the Holocaust and other atrocities:

> To the memory of those who were closest among the
> six million assassinated by the National Socialists, and
> of the millions on millions of all confessions and all
> nations, victims of the same hatred of the other man, the
> same anti-semitism.[1]

Here, Levinas sets those who were 'closest' to himself alongside the 'millions on millions' lost through the universalism of 'hatred of the other man' on an equal footing. The intimacy of friends and family does not privilege some against the many, but rather the otherness of each person privileges he or she in the context of all. The failure of receiving the Other with anything other than responsible care becomes a concrete complexity of atrocities during the war, which will always remain beyond understanding. This is what Michael Morgan calls that which is 'beyond thought'; the failure of Western culture, society, institutions and theories to realize goodness.[2] To reflect on it at all is to face the limits of what can be imagined. For Levinas, the Holocaust is both unique in its bureaucratic complexity and at the same time an example of the many large-scale horrors the world experienced in the same century. Tragically, the list of other examples is long. Familiar names like China's Cultural Revolution, Pol Pot's Cambodia or Stalin's purges conjure numbers among the millions. Alongside them are those less known to many, including the Congo at the beginning of the twentieth century, North Korea since the Korean War and the story of Rwanda in 1994. Each has its own unique cultural and historical circumstances, but the sheer scale of murder and torture is hard to stomach. After the Holocaust (indeed, after the twentieth century), evil confronts us not simply as an anxiety that is troubling, but also as an excess that cannot be understood. It burdens with a significance that goes beyond formal categories of reflection and transcends any means of worldly knowledge. In an essay on transcendence and evil, Levinas makes the point that evil manifests itself in an excessive quiddity seemingly transcendent to human experience.[3] It is a *something* which is beyond thought. As an excess that appears to be transcendent, evil makes itself known as that which is beyond meaning. In analysing the sense of evil as a presence open to investigation, Levinas brings discussion back to the notion of the Good and of God. In this sense, Levinas begins with the radical evil of an age that, at times, seems to have banished God and then describes his return.

Levinas draws from the Book of Job a dynamic between evil as excess and the awakening to God. In the perplexing story of Job, the Devil gambles over the limits of Job's faith and God seems to be complicit in suffering (see Job 1). One misery after another comes upon Job and still he remains faithful. In a way, the story becomes not an account of human faithfulness, but a tragic reflection on the mystery of evil and suffering in the face of an unknowable God. Despite sickness, death and every imaginable loss, the story returns again and again to the worship of God as he who cannot be explained or understood but to whom worship is owed: 'Behold, God is great, and we know him not; the number of his years is unsearchable' (Job 36:26). The worship of God is an interpretative key in which the mystery of God exceeds the human capacity to know and question him. The lamented figure of the narrative, the mysteriously faithful Job, has attracted attention far beyond the boundaries of Judaic-Christian thought. Indeed, the study of the Book of Job has a rich history, and it has provoked debate from the patristic era onwards.[4] Levinas draws his own inspiration from the work of Philippe Nemo, whose deep exegesis of the Book of Job is also permeated with philosophical questions.[5]

Nemo's study treats the Book of Job as an instructive personal narrative that reveals the emphatic incongruity between God or cosmic order and the experience of evil as an excessive reality. For Nemo, theodicies are by their nature impossible tasks in the face of radical evil. Levinas takes from Nemo three things:

First, he takes the role of anxiety in discussing evil. Anxiety is at the root of all social miseries and human dereliction.[6]

Second, because this anxiety is riddled through the experience of evil in the human condition, evil is also an excess. It exceeds not only understanding, but also experience.

The third feature is the strange intentionality of evil. It does not pervade human consciousness as a formless entity, but rather as an identification of one's own self. That is to say, evil has an intentionality and it is experienced in the self-directionality of a quality that seeks out the person and provokes it. Evil intends towards the oneself as a particular wounding, reaching the self, 'as though it sought me out'.[7] Evil points to the self and issues its identification of a 'you'.

In fact, the accusative naming of the oneself by otherness occurs in both the infliction of evil, and, as Levinas argues elsewhere, in God's address to Job: 'Where were you when I created the world?' (Job 38:4).[8] The question is, for Levinas, also a description of the responsibility Job has for all others in the world. If the self was not present at the beginning, he or she must locate one's responsible relationship to others at some other fixed moment of ethical importance. The implication is that one is immersed in a limited period of temporal responsibility; *this* is the epoch of one's responsibility, the period from one's birth to one's death. No other time has been given to the self. Standing before the divine Other, one stands accused and responsible in a localized space heavy with ethical signification. This is a form of accusation. Pain and suffering awaken the ego as an elected subject sought out in the action of accusation and persecution, as if a finger were pointed at the oneself. This fundamental experience shows itself for Levinas as the first difference (prior to the ontological difference), that of good and evil. For him, the first metaphysical question is not Gottfried Leibniz's 'why is there something rather than nothing?'[9] but rather, 'why is there evil rather than good?'[10]

The intentionality of evil is also a moment that reveals the horror of evil. Horror is a response to the ghastliness of an unwelcome threat to one's sensibilities. The assertion of a 'you' in the intentionality of evil provokes in the self a desire for that which opposes evil, what Levinas calls the 'expectation of the Good, of God and of a beatitude' that contrasts in measure to the excess of evil.[11] This is not a picture of simple opposition between good and evil which would make them comparable in power or significance. Or, alternatively, this is not the provocation of light against darkness. Rather, this opposition speaks of a surplus of the good over the excess of evil. God, it seems, is awakened as the active term in a thought process in which the very excesses and intentionality of evil issue a demand that there be a goodness greater than Being to overcome it. Good and evil are not spoken of as if the former could exact vengeance or retribution against the latter. This can be called a 'theophany', but only in the sense that beatitude always rises as an excess in surplus to the excess of evil.[12] The good is not the opposition to evil in a contested dialectic, but that which exceeds it.

Jean-Louis Chrétien has criticized Levinas' reading of the Job narrative and offers a theological alternative.[13] Chrétien argues that in the Book of Job, God directly asks Job the question as to where he was when the former laid the foundations of the world (Job 38:4)? Whereas Levinas interprets this to mean that God's voice implicates a tremendous responsibility upon the shoulders of Job, Chrétien objects that this places too complete a burden upon the human subject. God's question serves to distance the Creator from creatureliness, emphasizing the gulf between God who created the temporal-spatial world before human experience of it and the human person whose ethical responsibility is rather more limited. The role of 'supporter' of the universe is not given to Job in any absolute sense, but is maintained by God in his own privileged power.[14] Humility then would be a better mode of operation by which the human creature relates accurately to the sovereignty of a God who is absolutely Other. Furthermore, humility would better situate the fragile ethical responsibility held by each human subject in relation to both God and the excess of evil in the world.

The kind of evil that Levinas has in mind is that borne in the face of the other person. The evil that moves through the other person causes an effect like the breeze over a still lake; even at its most subtle there is a violence taking place. A ripple upsets the order of the water and reflection and light refract passively in the turbulence. The water is interrupted and inflicted with the presence of a natural force that is powerful, even when gently expressed. The lightness of the breeze may manifest itself subtly, but it remains a force that inflicts itself upon the water. It cannot be otherwise than an interruption. At its most excessive, violent storms offer the same image, with even more clarity. The 'original transcendence' of the Other inflicts the self with the provocation of a question, a touching of one's own private lament to self-enclosure.[15] In other words, this 'Good does not please, but commands and prescribes'.[16] In the meeting of the absolute Other with one's own self arrives the intentionality discussed above. Evil inflicts itself upon the Other and causes torment, and in so doing, the Other brings the question of evil to one's gaze and intensifies an interior desire for the Good. It is a Good that does not bring with it peace and concord, but demands the activity of justice and responsibility. Only in this way can beatitude overcome evil in any intelligible way. And moreover, the person is awakened once more not only to the Good in some thematizable measure of objectivity, as if that which is truly good could ever be adequately described, but rather the Good as the approach of a God who is infinite in possibility and whose movement towards the self is a proximity.[17] This experience of evil is not only that of the radical variety witnessed in the Holocaust, but also of evil as an excess that is present to typical human experience. What is experienced in day-to-day lives is often related to evil in some manner, whether perceived clearly or not. What is original in Levinas is the arrival of God in the perception of personal responsibility for the Other who is experiencing such evil. Furthermore, it is not a transcendent God who confirms a theodicy that captures and explains suffering. This would be to enclose suffering in a reasonable form or *logos*. No, suffering is diabolical and issues the demand of God's appearance, who, it is discovered, is proximate to one's personal responsibility for the Other.

In *Totality and Infinity* and *Otherwise than Being*, Levinas develops this relationship of divinity with the appearing of the

Other. In *Totality and Infinity*, Levinas makes little reference to God as such. Rather, divinity makes itself available to consciousness through the appearance of the Other. Specifically, the face is the occasion of God's presence: 'The dimension of the divine opens forth from the human face'.[18] Levinas speaks theologically of a philosophical assertion regarding that which is authentically transcendent. In the social relation to another human being, one is confronted with an ethical demand that speaks of both divinity and humanity in a transcendent dimension. Indeed, the Other is itself a transcendent that remains always beyond any formal description or logic, constituting a unique infinity.[19] Paradoxically, the transcendence of the Other is recognized not by that which surpasses categories of achievement, greatness or enterprise. Rather, it is in the 'destitution in the face of the Stranger, the widow, and the orphan' that otherness shows itself as transcendent to the self.[20] This allusion to the scriptural description of the needful other is connected with Levinas' description of God. Specifically, it is a reminder of the words of Zechariah 7:8-10:

> And the word of the Lord came to Zechariah, saying,
> "Thus says the Lord of hosts, Render true judgments,
> show kindness and mercy to one another, do not
> oppress the widow, the fatherless, the sojourner, or the
> poor; and let none of you devise evil against his brother
> in your heart."

The Word is given to Zechariah with the command to do good and to resist evil. The divine summons to resist evil is also an ethical demand. It places those of material need at the forefront of the divine mind and at the heart of an Old Testament *praxis* of obedience to Yahweh. Earlier, in Deuteronomy 10:18 it is written:

> He executes justice for the fatherless and the widow, and
> loves the sojourner, giving him food and clothing.

Again, the enjoinment of a divine command with a concrete ethics is an important biblical theme. This recurs in the Old Testament as a concrete disclosure of the kind of ethics God commands of his servants. It is one that takes its measure by the treatment of persons in need and anxiety, or those who pass our way as strangers on a different route. For Levinas, the image is important because the Other both solicits us and appeals to us. Old Testament texts cannot be read as a theoretical generalization, as if an ethereal category of widows and orphans ought to be cared for in some bland abstraction. The texts issue an ethical demand. They expect that attention be given to the singularity of 'the widow' and 'the orphan' as they actually appear. In so doing, the ethical demands of the particular Other are given in a unique needfulness. It is true that all widows and orphans require responsible care, but not all widows and orphans require the same kind of care at the same time. One widow requires bread, another warmth, another clean water. One requires swift attention and another requires long periods of time alone without intervention. The presence of God is not an abstracted originator of commands that echo across a distance into the theatre of human life, but instead is manifested within the face of the Other itself. It could be said that the realm of sociality is itself a form of theatre, but in Levinas, the script is issued within the dramatic structure of human life, rather than from a playwright standing apart from the stage.

For Levinas, there is no direct appearance of God, and only the direct correlation of God in the appearance of the Other, in whose face justice is demanded.[21] In such appearance, God rises as the 'correlative to the justice rendered unto men'.[22] The relationship of the face to divine presence maintains for Levinas the impossibility of thematizing God or circumscribing divinity into human comprehension. An incarnate moment of face-to-face sociality makes God visible even as it discloses the truth that God in Himself cannot be seen. Knowledge of God is located in the relationship of the oneself and the Other. Furthermore, the manifestation of the presence of God is described by Levinas as a 'height', the glory of which can be viewed as the metaphysical relationship.[23] In this way, metaphysics is constructed on the basis of the human relationship, which is a manifestation of supreme otherness. The needfulness of the widow, the stranger and the orphan elicits in the oneself the provocation of ethical responsibility that coincides with divinity.

A pause is called for at this point, because a theological difficulty arises in Levinas' account of God. It is not so much what Levinas affirms in the face-to-face that is problematic, but what he denies. Two terms are derided in his account, those of 'mediator' and 'participation'.[24]

In the first notion, mediation, Levinas refuses the possibility of the Other becoming a point of mediation (a 'mediator') between God (or any other) and the self. The irreducibility of the Other is such that otherness would be diminished if he or she were assigned the role of mediator. For Levinas, mediation would make the Other the incarnation of God, rather than the occasion of God's height and presence. In this schema, it is impossible to be an irreducible singularity of difference (the Other) while simultaneously mediating the presence of others. A strict distance is maintained between each other person and with God, so that no reduction of the Other to that which is mediated is possible. Indeed, the distance is not an ontological quantity, but a 'relocation' of divine attributes to the human person (e.g. infinity, revelation, glory, height, expiation and substitution).[25] The relocation of these divine attributes places an irreducible burden of singularity on each human person. Each other cannot be a mediation of God, as if the human-divine encounter depended on light filtering through a prism, but rather in God's 'trace', as the paradoxical mark of God's presence via his absence.[26] This is an integral feature of Levinas' wider project because its maintenance makes possible the primacy of the ethical in the irreducibility of the Other.

However, in Christian theology, mediation does not intrude on the irreducibility of the other person. An alternate trajectory occurs in the redemptive movement of a human being through *metanoia*, in which truth is mediated through the whole person. The turning of the self's orientation from sin to the grace offered in the person and work of Christ is both an entirely contingent activity (reliant on God's efficaciousness) and a liberating event (the person's more perfect self-authentication through salvation). The words of Christ promise both a mediatory gift and a radical disclosure of unique irreducibility:

> The thief comes only to steal and kill and destroy; I
> came that they may have life, and have it abundantly.
> (John 10:10)

Here, the promise of life is a fullness of experience each person may accept freely. In turn, the contrast with those who come only to thieve, kill and destroy confirms that Christ's words are not to reduce human persons by taking from them, but giving to them that which allows them to rise to new heights.[27] The forgiveness of the Christian tradition is offered freely and gratuitously, which manifests the person both interiorly and in its relationship with other persons and institutions. This is especially so in the Church, which is not yet the form of redeemed social and political life it is called to be.

John Milbank takes the ecclesiological dimension further. He argues that the ecclesia, because it is the body of Christ, mediates forgiveness itself.[28] Milbank describes the radical givenness of forgiveness in the Christian tradition as fundamentally a mediated gift in which personal integrity is strengthened. Christ's self-gift makes possible a human recognition of what is given in divine kenosis, and the integrity of communion through the Church is enabled: 'In dying, as God, he already receives back from us, through the Holy Spirit which elevates us into the life of the Trinity, our counter-gift of recognition'.[29] In other words, the Incarnation of the Son opens a new dimension of *communio* between human persons in the Spirit, who maintain their authentic humanity. An abundant life may be one in which mediation is possible, as long as it is founded on the gratuity of God's prior self-offering. If mediation merely refracts the presence of others through the person in the form of a passive conduit, then the Levinasian stricture on mediation would be ethically sound. In situations where this is manifested, then a Levinasian critique of that experience of mediation can indeed be fruitful. For example, the experience of those subject to violence and abuse in the home may afford us a glimpse of mediation in its debilitating form, of one person mediating a personal reduction in human dignity through the violence rendered towards another. Equally, relationships of unequal power may reflect the mediation of one person's will through the passive agency of a vulnerable counterpart, thus revealing a reduction in the singular dignity of another. This is further manifested when the victim feels obliged to lie to the exterior world, describing the relationship to others as peaceful and non-violent, when in fact he or she has become subjugated by another's power. Levinas provides tools with which to analyse these problems, but they do not adequately refuse the kind of mediation theologically rendered in Christ.

In the second term rejected by Levinas, that of participation, a crucial juncture is reached between theology and Levinas.[30] He denies that a direct comprehension of God is possible, although God is known in the face of the Other, who is absolutely other and transcendent.[31] The fruitfulness of the welcome offered to the human other who is in need (the widow, the orphan, the stranger etc) maintains a strict totality in its transcendental aspect. The other – always for Levinas the Other – is perfectly other to the oneself. As discussed above, it is in a perfect distance of two subjects of insurmountable difference that we find a manifestation of the divine. God's presence is located in the face-to-face. Levinas is concerned that the notion of participation in the divine might impede the otherness of the Other and the irreducible structure of that otherness. That is to say, the alterity manifested in the presence of the Other is to be conserved without immersing it in the presence of God. Levinas argues that the comprehension of God, 'taken as a participation in his sacred life, an allegedly direct comprehension, is impossible'.[32] For him, nothing is more immediate, direct and absolute than the face-to-face, in which two transcendent subjects meet across the traverse of infinite distance. In fact, it is never a true meeting, for alterity remains in every encounter. In the concept of participation, Levinas identifies a thematization and encompassing of the human subject as an object instead of the irreducible subject that issues an ethical demand.

Participation, in Levinas' interpretation, is a 'denial of the divine', because ethics itself cannot rely on the face of God, but on the manifestation of God in the face of the Other.[33] There is in Levinas a dissonance between the face of God and the self's participation in God's life. The former cannot be seen, whereas the latter would be a reduction in the legitimate alterity of the Other. A theology of participation that ignored Levinas' warning about the dangers of losing sight of the Other's alterity could quickly immerse the other person in a dehumanizing movement imposed from without. On the other hand, participation is an important aspect of soteriology and what the Eastern Orthodox tradition calls 'deification' or, in Patristic language, *theosis*. It would do well to consider what is meant by participation.

There is a long-standing theological purchase on the notion of participation. In the New Testament, an image of deification is put forward in the promise that disciples might 'become partakers of the divine nature' (2 Peter 1:4). In Christian self-understanding, the life of discipleship is one in which God's invitation to participate in the shared inner life of his grace and love is freely accepted. Henri de Lubac calls this, 'our participation, through the grace of Christ, in the internal life of the Divinity'.[34] This is a means of conceiving some share in the life of God, by virtue of God's first initiatory act of grace. Long preceding its various permutations among Catholic, Protestant and Eastern Orthodox theologians, a classic formulation of *theosis* is presented by the Bishop of Alexandria, St Athanasius (ca 296–373).[35] His treatise, *On the Incarnation* [*De Incarnatione*], remains an important account of the doctrine of God's Incarnation in the person of Jesus Christ, which was affirmed at the Council of Nicaea.[36] In it, Athanasius makes the startling statement that because the Son of God took human flesh, he opens the way for all humanity to participate in the Godhead. Athanasius states, 'He, indeed, assumed humanity that we might become God'.[37] This, in a truncated form, summarizes deification in the Christian tradition. Athanasius argues that the radical and singular event of divine incarnation – of Israel's God – in the person of Christ alters the drama of what it is to be a human being. With the perfect unity of two natures, divine and human, without reduction or detriment to the integrity of either, Christ promises his own divine glory to human flesh. This was the culmination of the biblical narrative, in which God's patience remained unwavering in the face of humanity's descent into sin and moral transgression, answering the brutish bestial nature of human flesh with the glory of the Incarnation.[38] This glory manifests itself in a recognizable body of human flesh and blood, thereby providing the means by which God can address and conjoin the corrupt nature in which all humanity shares, with the incorruptible nature of God.[39] It might be said that in the flesh of Christ, the bridge between corruptibility and incorruptibility is built and made steadfast. The importance of the Incarnation is of course deeply connected with the death and resurrection of Jesus Christ, in which the pledge and securing of salvation is made. While the early Christians maintained the strict monotheism they inherited as Jewish believers (it must be remembered that the first Christians were Jews), they developed a theology of the Trinity that held in tension the belief that God is both one and three. That God is one (see Deut 6:4) was never in doubt, but Athanasius played a pivotal role in defending the shared divinity of Christ with the Father (and indeed the Holy Spirit).[40] It is in the shared communion of Father, Son and Holy Spirit that Athanasius locates the object of divinization; the joyous participation in Christ's own person and the eternal progress of a deification of humanity. Athanasius defines this on the basis of Christ's Lordship, which is viewed in terms of its divine Sonship and Jesus' messianic role as the anointed one. To be united with Christ is to share in the life of the Trinity. This is of course a mystery and Athanasius cannot explain every aspect of the process. As one interpreter has put it, the theologian in this respect is far more concerned with explaining the salvific effects of Christ's radical presence in the flesh, than he is in developing the cause of those effects.[41] The point here is that a transformation is effected within the human person by virtue of the Incarnation, and there is no limitation on the freedom of the person or reduction in one's human nature. Freedom is indeed maintained to its fullest quality. The fullness of a demanding irreducible presence is maintained, and expanded as a sharer in the divine life.

This theme is a constant referent in the history of theology, and it confirms the place of participation in an account that is notably different from Levinas, or indeed in the kind of negative suggestions Levinas describes in participation as he sees it in Western thought generally. Other voices confirm this difference. St Augustine teaches that the directionality of God in descending to the world is what makes possible humanity's movement towards God.[42] The narrative is not one of humanity's reduction, but of its glory. The taking of human flesh is a confirmation by divinity of the opportunity by which human flesh may participate fruitfully in the being of God. Because the operation of grace depends fundamentally on the movement of God towards the world, and in the free adoption of human nature, it cannot be said that human persons are reduced in their nature or dignity by divine participation. For St Thomas Aquinas, the authority of Augustine is itself convincing:

> . . . the full participation of the Divinity, which is the
> true bliss of man and end of human life; and this is

bestowed upon us by Christ's humanity; for Augustine says in a sermon (xiii *de Temp*): *'God was made man, that man might be made God'*.[43]

The 'bliss' and 'end' of human life is, for Thomas and Augustine, a movement of becoming in the life of God. Humanity is no less human in this movement, but made more authentically human by virtue of participation in God, which is mediated through the person of Christ. Once again, participation, in this tradition, is not the reduction of the self against a totalizing presence of the divine, but rather the redemptive logic of grace as it operates within the human person in the context of the Triune life. It is through Christ's grace that such a communion of persons is made possible, just as the internal life of the Divinity does not subsume humanity, but welcomes and transforms it freely. The notion of participation as the substantive form of a grace-filled life has a number of permutations, and it should not be thought that there is only one understanding of it. Indeed, there has been a resurgence of interest in explaining its significance, such as investigations of Thomas Aquinas' understanding of metaphysical participation in creation, or the ecclesial participation of persons in *communio*.[44] The important point here is that Levinas' concern that the notion of divine participation is a diminishment of the Other is destabilized by Christian accounts of participation. The vision of human deification fits into neither Levinas' own conceptualization of participation nor the version he criticizes so strongly.

In *Otherwise than Being*, Levinas' account of divinity is not altered fundamentally. However, it is developed further in relation to what he calls the 'trace' of the infinite.[45] In the face of the Other resides an infinity of meaning and possibility which resides as a trace that comes from before and beyond time. It is not simply a trajectory of sense or awareness, but a signification regarding the Other in the realm of alterity. As such, the infinite shows itself in a kind of 'glory' that not only demands responsibility but also enacts the possibility of that responsibility.[46] Levinas' rhetorical language is an important feature of his poetic description of this responsibility, referring to the self being 'torn up' from its own beginning, the 'dispossession' of the self and its extraction from the concept in which 'I take refuge'.[47] The language reaches out, as it were, for a depiction of subjective experience that is not bound to a Cartesian vision of the world.[48] In this space of responsible action, the trace of God is witnessed. The trace must show itself in the glory of an absolute responsibility that acts as a witness to the Other. This trace is held in tension with what Levinas calls 'illeity', by which Levinas is speaking of a presence that commands, yet which is known precisely in its absence. This paradox draws from Plato and Plotinus and can be situated in a broad platonic approach, but maintains that the 'obliging character' of the face is itself the converging focus of the trace.[49] The face draws forth and the face commands, and in its character, the face bears the imprint of God, who has passed by in the epiphany of the Other. In its passing, the trace leaves no space for a theoretical structure in which to inhabit, or indeed for the self to make a commitment to the Other.[50] Even in acting for the Other, one is pointing towards the Other as a sign of privilege and eternal esteem. It is an infinite responsibility, not bound to any chronological account of perception and activity. As such, there is a sense in which the trace is from beyond time, representing the place in which God resides or which is prepared for God, but in which God is not so much seen as enacted. Having said that, the obligation towards the Other remains bound to the experience of temporality. As Michael Newman has argued, there is an emphasis then on the future as a break with the present and enjoinment with a non-recoverable past.[51] The trace, like God Himself, is always beyond Being and therefore beyond description, always evoking responsibility even as it makes possible that responsibility to begin with.

Here, it may be recalled that Levinas' philosophy is informed by his Jewish thought. While we cannot speak of the God of Abraham, Isaac and Jacob as if he could be contained within words and categories, the 'trace' Levinas describes evokes the presence of God as it appears to the Old Testament Patriarchs and Prophets. The burning bush (Ex 3:1-21) is an example. Here, Moses witnesses a fire that appears present before his eyes, yet does not consume the earthly material it resides in. Moses is commanded to remove his sandals and shield his eyes from the numinous divine display. It is from beyond time, and yet deferred to the strictures of time so that it might communicate with Moses. Yahweh identifies himself, and allows himself to be questioned by Moses. The trace appears to act humbly, but its power is great and its home is not among us. Yet it is also true that for Levinas, the appearance of God as a thought in the face of the Other makes possible a *language* about God. Levinas does not name it theology as such, but it is a theological language that appears. Some have argued that Levinas' theological language carries an atheistic accent. For Merold Westphal, Levinas' writing is atheistic in that the term 'God' is used without a strong adherence to its biblical meaning. As Westphal says, '[h]is God is not a Savior'.[52] Rather, God is associated with the trace that also serves to confirm the kind of subjectivity Levinas identifies in human consciousness. That is, one that experiences a certain calamity within its own existentiality and out of which it cannot move in its own strength. This calamity is, for Levinas, essentially atheistic.

It is important to recognize that Levinas does not mean by this term the end of theistic belief, or any form of rebellious denial of one's own religious heritage. Atheism, for Levinas, is the state of existence that is prior to either affirmation or denial of the existence of God. Edith Wyschogrod views it as the ground against which revelation becomes possible and is, therefore, a kind of innocence that Levinas views (despite our otherwise calamity) in the human condition.[53] What Wyschogrod here calls 'atheistic man' is the state of human being prior to the advent of the Other. It is the human condition *prior* to its command to act, and therefore innocent of condemnation because it cannot yet be judged. One must be commanded before one is judged. And one must be judged before one can be condemned. Atheistic man is that state of existence anterior to the commandment of the Other to act for the Other. For Levinas, theism is the idea of the infinite as it is cognitively apprehended. Because this follows a formal process within the human subject, atheism is a normative condition to which theism relates as an addendum that does not alter the human subject's fundamental existentiality. One might suggest that atheism is a term Levinas uses for the human condition, rather than as a religious or ideological choice. One is not an atheist; one's condition is atheistic. It is because of this approach to the human condition that Levinas can make the claim that the appearance of the Other person is the event of divinity's appearance before the self.

For Wyschogrod, this is the point at which atheistic man is interrupted by the divinity of the face of the Other purged of all myths. Atheistic man is woken up, sobered up, pointed in the direction of the glaring light of alterity and made to see his accuser in the face of the Other. The challenge for theology is not this event *per se*, but Levinas' description of this event as the only moment in which a divine access occurs, direct and non-participatory. As Wyschogrod argues, [t]he metaphysical relation, the idea of the infinite, ties us to the holy without sacralizing the self through participation in a *numinosum*'.[54] This tying to the holy is a form of relational binding, in which holiness demands an ethical response rather than a personal encounter such as classical religious language might describe. It is, as Wyschogrod further elaborates, an atheism in which the God of positive religions is not the domain of mythic participation, but a category of terms from which the 'absolute' can be disengaged for the service of ethics. Wyschogrod rightly sees the significant departure that Levinas invokes in what he calls mythic language from an experience of the sacred.

Fundamentally, the sacred, for Levinas, rises in the gleam of the face of the Other. God is the condition for a just rendering of one to the Other, and he is also the enactment of justice as it is experienced. Yet, in a complex way, he is not restricted to either of these categories. Wyschogrod calls Levinas' God a fixed point outside of society, from whence justice comes.[55] He appears to be more than the sum of human endeavour, while not known outside the realm of inter-subjectivity. He cannot be thought outside of the existence of the third person who interrupts the relation of the oneself and the other, thus constituting the upsurge in which the singularity of each of the two is unsettled and called outside of itself, revealing the complex web of relationships that converge in society at large. Levinas relies profoundly on the return of this language for a divinity that seems to unfold all ethical possibilities for social contexts. Because it is far-ranging, it can be all too fragile. It would be easy to formulate Levinas' God-language as a simple occurrence of divinity in sociality without regard for the intricate balance he attempts. Yet the various theological terms he incorporates in his philosophy require attentiveness and constant return to his own texts. His argument follows a complex line of reasoning (if it can be called reason; it reads more like an appeal or a demand than an argument), even if its application is intended to be immediate and non-reflective. This is recognized by Jeffrey Bloechl who argues that the response to the face is a commitment to a radical and infinite responsibility 'without qualification'.[56] The divinity that demands such an absolute response is not a classical notion of God from either Jewish or Christian traditions, but nor is it necessarily antithetical to either. It relies on Levinas' redefinition of terms such as atheism, divinity and God.

Levinas' account of the term 'God' is, therefore, an important feature of his entire reconstruction of philosophy. On the one hand, it is a common word in his texts, invoking the kind of height and glory he finds in both the Hebrew Scriptures and in the event of alterity in the other person. On the other hand, its definition has occasionally shifted, at times seeming to indicate the Jewish notion of the God who reveals Himself as a being outside of Being, but at others as merely a philosophical construct designed to convey a truth discovered in phenomenology. Levinas explores how the term might be understood in the collection titled, *Of God Who Comes to Mind*.[57] These 13 essays interrogate the possibilities of understanding the significance of the word 'God', largely in a phenomenological setting.

A crucial essay is entitled *God and Philosophy*, and here Levinas makes a severe criticism of theology. Levinas outlines the broad possibility of authentic philosophy, and the problem, for him, with revealed theology. Levinas enters the context of Western philosophical discourse with the opening words, 'Not to philosophize is still to philosophize'.[58] He writes with an awareness of the kinds of problems being opened up by thinkers such as Jacques Derrida, for whom a deconstructive tendency was challenging the heart of philosophy. Levinas views in Western philosophy the coincidence between the thought and the reality in which this thought thinks. This is the realist situation that for Levinas is deeply problematic when the term 'God' is used. For him, the biblical notion of God has a significance that lies beyond Western philosophical categories, for it cannot be contained or limited by them. For Levinas, this limitation is precisely what the Greek mind attempted when it 'thought' God, resulting in a destruction of transcendence. In being 'thought', God became situated within the 'gesture of being', and so theology themetized God in a reduction of what was beyond Being to the level of constructed ontology. Levinas argues:

> Rational theology, fundamentally ontological, endeavors to accommodate transcendence within the domain of being by expressing it with adverbs of height applied to the verb "to be." God is said to exist eminently or *par excellence*. But does the height, or the height above all height, which is thus expressed still depend on ontology?[59]

Here, Levinas makes a fundamental claim about the movement of biblical faith, through Christianity, into Greek philosophy.

If true, it is a devastating claim to make. Levinas describes transcendence as an accommodation within Being, and therefore as a denial of the biblical notion of God. He questions whether the height of the glory of essential Being seen in God is indeed what the theologians intended, or whether it has become something other. The *esse* about which Levinas questions is, for him, unintelligible, even within the language of perfect otherness. Opposed to this is Levinas' conceptualization of biblical faith, for which ontology is to be rebuked profoundly. He argues that, '[n]othing is less opposed to ontology than the opinion of faith'.[60] It is here that Levinas invokes a scepticism not simply of the role of Being in conceiving of the truth of human existence, but of the Western approach to knowledge as such. Levinas inverts a classical understanding of knowledge. Instead of thought and experience being viewed as a reflection of exteriority in an inner forum, he argues that it may only ever comprehend itself 'in its own essence, starting from consciousness'.[61] This is a move towards subjectivity as the context in which consciousness assembles a knowledge of itself. It is not inspired within its own interiority to assemble such knowledge. Rather, it is the experience of the self as 'the Same' who is provoked by the Other to attend to the need of the Other.[62] Levinas likens this experience of knowledge as a consciousness marked by the quality of *insomnia*, in which the self is attuned to a knowledge that refuses self or rest. An infinity of possibility arises in this intense, draining wakefulness, which allows for the idea of God without recourse to Being *qua* being.

Levinas wants to re-establish the possibility of the term 'God' in philosophical discourse, without relying on ontology. As such, it is an experiential moment in which such a term becomes alive, and one that carries a primarily ethical content. Levinas views the appropriate posture before the biblical notion of God as one who stands accused, humbled before the advent of an alterity over which no categories or descriptive terms can hold power. The Other *is* the authoritative one who vestiges the self in responsibility. Levinas quotes Dostoevsky's *The Brothers Karamazov*: 'Each of us is guilty before everyone, for everyone and for everything, and I more than the others'.[63] Responsibility is an excess that moves thought outside of the strictures of Being. Furthermore, the divine Other is one who disturbs the self out of sleep and by consequence, out of the event of dreaming. Fantasies are put to flight and the language of *mythos* and imaginative narratives are put out of one's mind. They have no place in the return of God for Levinas' philosophy. Once again, the image of waking up, or indeed, sobering up, is used repeatedly. They serve the metaphor of insomnia by viewing the latter as a state of Being, whereas one must follow a process to reach this moment of experience. The return of God is a philosophical moment in which the idea of divinity rises in the subjective moment of alterity, and the only appropriate response is to maintain a wakeful vigilance. Because this is primarily an ethical moment and not an intellectual or reflective moment, Levinas closes his essay by overturning his opening statement. He restates it thus: 'Not to philosophize would not be still to philosophize'.[64] God's return disallows the overarching philosophical position in which the opening statement could be uttered. It insists that the human person be open to a means of conceiving itself and others without the limitations of an ontology that denies difference and ethical responsibility. It is a fissure in existence and a moment of transcendence that interrupts its own phenomenality, as Levinas describes. There is a disturbance that occurs in this movement of Levinas' philosophical understanding of the biblical God, one that signifies the self as a servant and destabilizes Levinas' own concept of the role of theology in relation to philosophy.

It is destabilized largely because Levinas' account of Western philosophy is so markedly bound up with an onto-theology, that is to say, a conceptualization of Being in which God remains a theological construct that is limited by ontology. The advent of the thought of God, once more, as it were, requires a significant reconstruction if Levinas' God-talk is to be enacted successfully. Elsewhere, Levinas takes up this theme and speaks of a going beyond the world and listening to a voice more intimate than intimacy.[65] He begins with Husserlian intentionality, assuming a unidirectionality of the movement of knowledge, but puts it aside to emphasize what he calls 'a deference' to God through phenomenology. In the phenomenality of the appearance of the Other, God acts as a point of de-ferring intentionality that allows an intimate voice to speak from within the interiority of subjective experience. Levinas refers strikingly to Søren Kierkegaard, in whom he finds a thinker who recognizes the role of an uncertain spirit before the trembling gravity of divinity. For Kierkegaard, as for Levinas, this trembling is manifested as a result of the perception of an authentically absolute difference between oneself and the Other.[66] Levinas revels in the diminutive distance of that which we cannot know for certain. The modes of seeking, suffering and questioning are open embraces of the alterity that draws near to the self in the form of the divine. The return of God is not the advent of uncertainty, but the comfort drawn in the subjective moment in which it is recognized that not all of reality is open to one's gaze. Rather, the Other opens up all of reality as a life to be lived responsibly, and as a vigil to be observed and felt. Nevertheless, it must be repeated: for Levinas, the other person is not God, and nor is God the great Other in the strictly horizontal relationship in which transcendence is produced.[67] Levinas' strong rejection of these associations do not of course make the category of God a simple description, but it does clarify somewhat what God, for Levinas, is not. The return of God does reconstruct the relationship between theology and philosophy, by seeking to moor them both to an alterity that cannot be restricted or described in full.

As this chapter began, it was argued that Levinas perceived in the Holocaust a historical event that was experienced as unique. Its horror is etched in the social imagination as unique for its bureaucratic efficiency and universal objectives. It was an attempt at eradicating an entire race. Moreover, the race it sought to exterminate was a people who perceived themselves as the historical people of God, a community that, for Christians, manifests in its holy texts and tradition a historical narrative of human–divine interaction. After the Shoah, Levinas asks whether the term 'God' is of any use. Remarkably, he responds with a resounding affirmation of its appropriateness, but only within the stable of human inter-subjectivity. For example, the cry of dereliction in Job does not deny God, but affirms the necessity of a singular, demanding alterity that seeks out authentic justice. While Job's wife asks if he would keep his integrity despite his many sufferings and exasperates, 'curse God and die!' (Job 2:9), Job Himself relents in the lonely path of faithfulness. The truth is that faithfulness becomes its own reward. While the book concludes with a material wealth presented to Job, this was not a gift that recompenses Job for his sickness, his poverty or, worse still, the abandonment of his friends. The final words indicate that Job lived into a great age, 'full of days' (Job 14:17) and with the joys of beautiful children and grandchildren. Time itself becomes a gift to Job from the creator of time and space.

For Levinas, the gift of Job is of a testament to the surprising event of God in the face of evil as an excess. Levinas indicates that evil is experienced as a quiddity – an *itness* – in which a substantial presence is felt. If left there, it could be argued that Levinas' theodicy formally contends a material essence to evil, thus rejecting the tradition of thinkers like Augustine, for whom evil is characterized by a certain lack within the created order.[68] For Augustine, evil is a privation of the good within the world, a *privatio boni*. It is marked chiefly by its lack within creation and therefore not so much a turning towards a substance, as a turning away from the higher good. This occurs within the will in which it is revealed that an inner defection is at work in the evil action itself. Yet Levinas' account of evil is not constructed to argue for an essence or a substance in which evil is recognized, but rather to argue for its substantial nature as an event that is experienced. Within the human condition, evil acts as an intentionality that seeks the self out and manifests a performance that ends in suffering. Evil may or may not have a substance, but it is felt as a powerful quiddity. As such, it is also an excess that overflows human attempts to form an adequate answer. In fact, this is why Levinas' account is not so much a theodicy as an anti-theodicy; a theory as to why theorizing about evil is impossible. No thought can contain or limit evil within its parameters. In Levinas' account of Job, this excess provokes a surprising reaction, in that the thought of God is made possible. A powerful human response is the subjective experience of divine resistance against evil. It is not necessarily an experience that is felt or witnessed at all times. The human person must become more profoundly aware of it, and follow its logic with more faithful reflection. For Levinas, it rises up in the face of evil and the only appropriate language is, essentially, the language of God-talk. Evil provokes and calls out from the human person the search for God as one who resists, corrects and overcomes evil. This is echoed multiple times in Levinas' essay on transcendence and evil, which he opens with words from Isaiah:

> I establish peace and am the author of Evil,
> I, the Eternal, do all that. (Isaiah 45:7)

God is the author of all, and so the good that might be achieved in the face of evil is a true good, to which the name of the divine can be attached. Levinas approaches evil as a phenomenological moment in which the human person discovers he or she is not bound to Being as such. The true binding, for Levinas, is to the authenticating *modus operandi* of responding well to the suffering Other. It is the act of caring in the fullness of time for the other person that a true solidarity with those who experience evil is felt. For Christians, a more complete picture of the cry of dereliction is given in Christ upon the Cross.[69] In what are known as the seven last words from the cross, Jesus of Nazareth makes a number of brief, but theologically rich statements (called so for the seven sayings completed during the crucifixion and recorded across three of the Gospels). The fourth saying is a quotation from Psalm 22 known as the Word of Abandonment: 'My God, my God, why hast thou forsaken me' (Matt 27:46 and Mk 15:34). Here, one can also see the abjectly human question of the one who suffers excruciating torment. The figure of Christ is an innocent scapegoat; tortured, abandoned, made to bleed for others. For his disciples, this is as full an image of human dereliction as can be imagined. In thinking through this narrative with Levinas, one must recall the latter's notion that it is not excessive evil as such, that makes possible the thought of God once more.[70] Rather, it is the notion of evil as an excess. In the figure of Christ, both can be seen. On the one hand, an excessive evil is present in that a perfect injustice is rendered unto one who is innocent of the sins for which he pays a price. This is one who has preached the kingdom of God publicly and who healed the sick and shared a message of good news among the poor and the downtrodden. On the other hand, the evil that is done to Christ is the shared burden of every innocent person, and indeed, the punishment of the cross was inflicted on countless other convicts under Roman rule. The flogging and the public shame Christ experiences in the passion are hardly unique to him. In every generation there are those who suffer similar fates somewhere upon the face of the earth. In this way, it can be seen that Christ's suffering is both singularly extraordinary and utterly banal. Over the course of history, the claims made of Jesus are of a messianic figure who enfolds within his own personal narrative both the hope of one who might suffer for our misdeeds and of one who experiences human nature with the subjective content of every other person who suffers through the intentional evil of others. The Levinasian analysis is helpful for clarifying the role of evil-as-excess, and shows further the uniqueness of claims about the person of Christ. It confirms the appropriateness of a self-kenosis that opens itself up as the suffering in which the self suffers further for devotion that seems nonsensical to a faithless world. The words of St Paul are of course relevant: 'Now I rejoice in my sufferings for your sake, and in my flesh I am filling up what is lacking in Christ's afflictions for the sake of his body, that is, the church' (Col 1:24). Though Christ's suffering is complete, it remains to be rendered in each other human subjective moment. Of course, for Levinas, the difference between God – the Infinite – and the human is of such absoluteness that it remains always non-correlative. And furthermore, for Levinas, the interruption of the alterity of the Other breaks up the sameness ('the Same') with an ethical possibility that remains both a divine thought and a responsibility that cannot be refused:

> Ethics requires a subject bearing everything, subjected to everything, obedient with an obedience that precedes all understanding and all listening to the command. Therein lies a reversal of heteronomy into autonomy, and this is the way in which the Infinite comes to pass.[71]

For Levinas, an authentic ethics breaks open the truth of humanity as a subjective moment that reinterprets all experience. Yet, theological reflection centres upon the figure of Christ in the paradoxical insistence that in his passion, glory passed through the human narrative. The call of Levinas, that an authentic ethics is a supreme passivity of obedient responsibility, is confirmed and concretized in the event of Christ.

In conclusion, Levinas allows for a philosophical reconstruction of the conceptualization of God in contemporary thought. It relies profoundly on theological language to achieve such an audacious goal, but is oriented by the historical event of the Holocaust. In the terrible events of that period, the Jewish people – including Levinas' family, friends and colleagues – experienced the horror of an intended extermination. It was the decimation of the other under the management of an efficient bureaucracy that was not halted by European

Christianity, despite various heroic and saintly attempts to do so. After the Holocaust, how may God be thought or spoken of? And what purpose does philosophy serve if its handling of the term God is complicated by notions of Being that are unhelpful to a concrete practice of justice?

First, Levinas' work re-conceives of the notion of God first as a thought that rises. It moves upwards in the sense of an ethical height because it is an infinity derived in the face-to-face alterity of the self recognizing the otherness of the Other.

Second, the correlation of the Scriptures with the self-identify of the modern state of Israel is both fruitful, and difficult to sustain. History speaks against such a close relationship between theology and politics, and Levinas' biblical heritage upsets this alliance.

Third, the Other is rendered disincarnate by Levinas. While the level of responsibility he identifies before the other can be attractive for theology, alterity itself is absolute to the degree that the uniqueness and the particularism of each human person is diminished.

Fourth, Levinas relies on theological language without interpreting it according to traditional theological constructs. Specifically, Levinas denies in the divinity of the Other the terms 'mediation' or 'participation', and this is deeply problematic, because Levinas does not engage with the unique manner in which Christian thought understands those terms to operate.

Fifth, in the face of the Other, the holy and the sacred make their appearance. There are no holy places, shrines or liturgies in Levinas, at least not according to his account of the sheer magnitude of what occurs in the face-to-face.

Sixth, the return of God invokes in the self an insomnia before alterity. The oneself is awakened to the driving necessity to act for the Other and meet the need of the Other.

This is a strong account of the ethics of alterity, perhaps too strong to bear. In it, God rises and accuses the self and one must act humbly before a subjective glory in the gleam of the face.

It has the capacity to return thought to the idea of infinity, and in this it offers great promise. But the theologian must be careful not to conflate Levinas' theological language with the language of faith as a particular tradition might define it. Indeed, the driven necessity to return to the texts and define terms must be achieved carefully. But Levinas' claim that 'God' might be a significant biblical term for philosophy and for authentic ethics cannot be ignored. We would ignore such an argument at our peril, for in a secular age in which religious language is rendered incoherent, Levinas is nuanced, rigorous and counter-intuitive. Now, this does not render God's return as such. Rather, it is a philosophical analysis that concludes in the conviction that God was never made absent, and that we have need for a return of appropriate language that renders this truth clearly and ethically. In other words, 'God' never made a departure. In response to this discovery, language and philosophy return to a presence that accentuates the good in an ethical responsibility that is limitless, because the divine thought itself is an infinity.

Chapter 7
Conclusion

The work of Emmanuel Levinas is a gift for theology. It provokes theological practitioners to reflect carefully upon the ethical nature of their work, and the demand made in the face of the other person. Yet such a statement cannot be made without qualification, for the gift of Levinas is not one of easy self-assurance, but its very disturbance. Throughout this book, it has been argued that the encounter of theology with Levinas provokes theology towards self-inspection and philosophical renewal. It informs the theologian with rich discoveries of a phenomenology of inter-subjectivity, without falling into a simplistic negation of the objective content of Revelation.

Indeed, because the theologian begins with God, he or she voyages in the realm of thought with an objective category that refuses a simple enfolding within subjectivity. Such a God, for Christian theologians, has extended his self-revelation through the dynamism of the human body, incarnating divinity in the subjective narrative of a man in history. The dogmatic content of this claim sits at the heart of the vocation of the theologian – reflecting, explaining, teaching, understanding, inculcating it – all the while surveying contemporary debate in the search for language that might convey the dogmatic content of the Church's faith adequately and accurately. In this way, the theologian is faced with a divine alterity that, while drawing near in the person of Christ, remains radically distinct from human experience and the Creation itself. The gift of Levinas is to craft a language that is of use in this vocational paradox. It is not that Levinas' thought is readily conducive to theology as a *praeparatio evangelica*. No, it is rather that Levinas' phenomenological language of alterity and the dramatic ethical content of the face-to-face open a space in which the theologian may once more speak of God in the world as it is experienced. And the language used to speak of God is, at a fundamental level, one that is *given* to the theologian. The provocation of Levinas spoken of in Chapter 1 of this book is not simply to rethink Western philosophy and its approach to Being as such, but to provocatively stir up the recognition of responsibility in the face of alterity.

In Chapter 2, the contours of this provocation were explored as they permeate the work of Levinas' two most substantial contributions, *Totality and Infinity* and *Otherwise than Being: or Beyond Essence*. Levinas argues that ontology has displaced the event of difference between persons, and this is to the detriment of authentic ethical responses to otherness. Because Being is approached as an ontologization of existence, it results in a primacy of categories, absolute borders and the decimation of an adequate recognition of the unique face of the Other. Indeed, the visage of the Other is itself displaced, precisely because it is described and located within the horizon of Being. It was argued that Levinas does not intend the end of a philosophy of Being, but rather its dramatic reconstruction informed by the event of alterity. It was also argued that this provocative stance of Levinas is not of moral outrage or the cry of the prophet, but that of the 'philosopher's lament'. By this, I mean to convey the notion that Levinas is attempting to philosophize about human existence, and not to preach or moralize. He leaves such tasks to others. Of course, the phenomenological description of the needful Other renders us incapable of anything but care and responsibility, and there is no doubt that Levinas intends that much at least. But he is not seeking out an affective response or something like guilt in his description of responsibility. It is instead an appreciation of responsibility as a hard fact, or like the iconic language utilized by Jean-Luc Marion, it remains fixed and certain, seeming to gaze at the self and issue a judgement upon one's failures before the suffering Other.

Now, the event of Jesus Christ fulfils the iconic role that Marion takes from Levinas, and thwarts the tendency to conceptual limitation within God-language. The sheer givenness of the Christ, whose messianic character takes him all the way to the cross and to the other side of death, is always a self-givenness. He is self-directed in the same moment in which he is directed towards the Father; self-revealing, and strangely motivated not in a self-love as such, but in a love for his own other; the human person and all of Creation. The stirring descriptions of the face-to-face in Levinas, both in his major works and in so many other of his published writings, constitute an attempt to locate an incarnate moment of authentic ethical awareness. The Levinasian description of such a moment has constant recourse to language that theologians will recognize to a marked degree, especially concerning God and infinity. And, as I have argued, this does not contradict the Christian notion of Incarnation, but confirms its significance for theologians who ought to feel some chastisement should they discover that Incarnation has not played the central role in their thought that it is owed.

Of course, Levinas himself was not a theologian. He was suspicious of Christian theology and expressed a distaste for any sudden leap from his phenomenology to the God of revelation. This must be remembered at all times. Any simplistic association of the latter with the former is to enter murky conceptual waters and to take the risk of an unfruitful onto-theology. In the contemporary debate about the 'theological turn' discussed in Chapter 3, it can be seen that Levinas stands at the convergence of multiple currents; a plurality of Husserlian interpretations will adopt or reject Levinas for their own projects, his use of theological terms and even phraseology offends some and entices others, and the semi-mystical language of Levinas itself reflects various influences, including the broader Rabbinic tradition, Platonic philosophy and the Hebrew Scriptures. It is of no help to thread Levinas uncritically into a new pattern of phenomenological discourse, or to inculcate his work simplistically into a contemporary agenda, be it philosophical, theological or otherwise. Rather, his thought can stand on its own, and it warrants critical attention because of its universal application. For Levinas, alterity elects the self in an ethical vocation that is rigorous and absolute. *I* am responsible for *everyone* else *all* of the time. It seems too much to bear. Indeed, the self cannot achieve that which such an ethical venture calls it to enact. The transcendent nature of the ethical call of alterity is a difficult election. For this reason, theology has a role to play in answering the election precisely from the context that Levinas was so suspicious of; ecclesial space. The absolute responsibility that Levinas notes in his descriptions of the face-to-face is recognized by Christian tradition as a vocation that is mediated through holy texts. The Scriptures speak of the election of those who responded to a simple voice, not apart from the world but within it. The surplus of meaning in the inter-human election of one person before the Other requires the theologian to recognize that the work of theology is itself a task already being completed before pen is put to paper. It is being written in the relationship of one person to another and in the call of the Other towards the self. Responsibility for others is a divine election.

This leads to an examination of the manner in which theology is implicated in Levinas' reappraisal of the ethical relationship. Some time was spent in taking up the concept of 'God' as an idea that rises in the event of Being and transcends it. The divine infinity rises in judgement upon the self, shines a light upon its fractious relationship with the world, and calls it out of its own self for the sake of others. 'God', for Levinas, is 'other otherwise' and 'transcendent to the point of absence'.[1] For Levinas, 'God' is a meaningless term unless it authenticates a 'beyond' Being. The tendency to onto-theology is for Levinas a dangerous movement of philosophical reflection, for it circumvents the authority of the divine names to inculcate a genuine awareness of ethical responsibility. It might be suggested that God becomes a restrictive word among other words. Instead, Levinas' conceptualization of God is a surplus of meaning that sits above human rationality and endorses only care and wisdom as they offer themselves up for the suffering Other. I have taken from Levinas this fruitful outline of the category of 'God', but developed it in the light of approaches to 'prayer' in both the Old and the New Testaments, and Levinas' own reflections upon the term. Increasingly it seems to me that Levinas opens a way for theology to exert its energies as itself an ethical expression of prayer, while not relinquishing its ancient claim to be, as St Anselm famously put it, '*fides quaerens intellectum*'.[2] Such prayer is more than contemplation, although it may begin there. It is also the response to suffering as it is witnessed in Creation. What is hoped for in prayer (the glory of God) is enacted by tending to others, in whose own incarnate existence is witnessed God's trace. Prayer then is not the resting of the spirit, but the restless spirit seeking out the rest of God and of others. It is written through with an ethical regard for the face of the Other because, as Levinas puts it, the 'ethical must intervene!'[3] And after all, as Chapter 4 also argued, theology finds itself not sealed off from the world, but gazed upon by the suffering Other and awakened to its own nakedness and shame. Theology is not itself a glory, but a task in which the Other is glorified.

This book is written by an author who understands himself to be a practitioner of the Christian faith. This is done self-reflectively and, it is hoped, self-critically. Theology within that tradition is never the product of an individual or a select few. It is a task performed on behalf of a wider ecclesial context – of the Church – and is called constantly to renew itself within this embodied community. Despite many troubling episodes of history, there has been, as part of that renewal, an attempt to renew the best possible relations between Christians and Jews, which includes an intellectual and spiritual encounter between thinkers of both traditions. For example, Levinas was a friend and guest of Pope John Paul II on numerous occasions, and the latter described him as one of the 'philosophers of dialogue', who, alongside Paul Ricœur and Martin Buber, offers profound insight into the symbolic and metaphysical textures of the Bible.[4] In Chapter 5 of this book, it has been seen how Levinas' account of Israel's faith is a demanding self-abnegation, held in tension within the community of God's people. Levinas describes a preference for the 'shadows' of Jewish texts and questions, rather than the glare and light of the Gentile world. In particular, he appreciates the vital truths present in the ambiguities and challenges of his religious tradition over and against the self-contained totalities he identifies in Western thought outside the Jewish fold. In the shadows of those ambiguities is a moral strength to remain humble before God's revelation and before a world that bears itself up proudly and arrogantly. This is what Levinas also calls the 'little faith' of Israel.[5] It is not that he rejects the truths of the Gentiles *per se*, but that Israel is obliged to strip itself of the world's pomposity and give time to the reading and studying of its sacred texts. This is an approach drawn out by Levinas which Christians and others may learn from. There remains always in Levinas a lively relationship between holy texts and the rendering of justice in the world, and of a concrete ethics that is universal by virtue of its personal election in every person. Such a relationship allows for the practice of ethics to be, for those of faith, contingent upon an adequate reading of the Scriptures.

Nevertheless, a problematic aspect of Levinas' appreciation for the shadows is in his account of the political expression of the 'little faith'. Levinas defends a strong relationship between the modern State of Israel and its religious roots in the Hebrew Scriptures. As it was argued, Levinas' claim tempts fate, in that the policies of the statist expression of Israel may well (and some have argued have already) fundamentally break from what is taught in the Scriptures at hand. Perhaps it is simply that Levinas hopes for too much? If he does, there is a subtle naivety at work, and one would do well to take up the kinds of rigorous suspicion he affords politics in other texts. In fact, a lesson can be learnt here by Christians who may wish for a formal political expression of their faith (and there are many). History is no friend in this regard, and the intellectual line of argument that defends a robust relationship between political and statist structures and holy texts too easily weds a faith to the spirit of the age. The latter will pass and the former will be anchorless in a vast sea. In a way, Levinas is most informative for Christian theologians when he speaks of the vocation of the Jewish people as a source of light to the world. This vocational aspect of the Jewish people stands above history, even as it enters history in every epoch. It links the activity of justice in the world to the un-tamed God of Israel, who is unbound to the category of Being as the Greeks would have it. This results in a concretized justice that entices, instructs and develops authentic community. This account cannot be understood apart from Levinas' reading of the Scriptures, and because of its intimacy between the holy texts and ethics, offers a means also of understanding the Christian ecclesia in the contemporary moment. If a true ethics finds its impetus in the disclosure of Scripture within the communion of God's people, then Christians may find in Levinas a developed account of how texts are to speak, and how their shadows are to be appreciated humbly and justly.

In Chapter 6, we returned to the question of 'God' and to the context of the Holocaust. This is significant, for we live in a secular age and in a time of new holocausts. Waves of horror ripple through peoples of the world no less than in the past, and we remain as bereft as ever as to how permanent change might be enacted. And the Holocaust of World War II continues to permeate history as a particularly large-scale 'hatred of the other man', of an anti-Semitism that was bureaucratic and efficient, and which continues to raise questions about Europe and its identity. That Levinas, having witnessed the Holocaust and lost intimate companions to it, might turn to the category of 'God' in his philosophy ought to be a striking aspect of his corpus. And he achieves something further because in the rising, once more, of 'God', Levinas establishes a philosophical language that opens the way for theological language to enter calmly and soberly. This is not the conflation of Levinas' 'God' with the God of the Old or the New Testaments in an intellectual sleight of hand, but of the development of a language that recognizes a simple truth in the complexities of human experience. It looks soberly at the inter-subjective moment, and recognizes that God and God-talk is not made inappropriate by evil in the world. Moreover, human suffering does not require the quiet exit of God from the human stage, as if misery and pain held such totalizing power. Rather, Levinas shows that the significance of the biblical vision of God and the discovery of theological language to explain even the idea of infinity renders theology a crucial part in an account of human existence.

Therefore, it may be said with confidence that the theologian finds encouragement in the rigours of Levinas' thought. In Levinas, the theologian discerns an attentiveness to the other person that is manifest in a language that privileges categories he or she ought to be familiar with: God, infinity and glory. In Levinas, one comes across an approach to incarnation that is both highly fruitful and, admittedly, problematic. For example, the insights of Levinas on the nature of responsibility and the living relationship between holy texts and a concretized justice are richly counter-cultural but, on the other hand, Levinas seems to miss altogether the nature of participation and mediation as Christian tradition has perceived them, constituting a space in the dialogue between Christianity and Judaism. In relation to Levinas' account of incarnate existence in all its ambiguities, the language of divine Incarnation in its dogmatic light has a significance that theologians would do well to take up with sustained regard. Despite these various convergences in Levinas, the struggle that one enacts in reading him − across all the genres in which he wrote – is fruitful fundamentally because it returns the enquiring mind to three crucial aspects of the task of the theologian: the radical vocation engendered in divine election, the unremitting relationship between sacred Scripture and the practice of justice in the world, and a renewed perception that theology is an ethical task performed within the fullness of communion with others.

Notes

Chapter 1

1. Brague (1995). 'The Impotence of the Word: The God Who has Said It *All.*' *Diogenes* 43/2(170): 45.
2. Malka (2006). *Emmanuel Levinas: His Life and Legacy.* Pittsburgh: Duquesne University Press, 6.
3. Levinas (2001). *Is it Righteous to Be?: Interviews with Emmanuel Levinas.* Stanford: Stanford University Press, 28.
4. Critchley and Bernasconi (2002). *The Cambridge Companion to Levinas.* Cambridge: Cambridge University Press, xvii.
5. See Levinas (2003). *De l'évasion: On Escape.* Stanford: Stanford University Press.
6. Critchley and Bernasconi (2002). *The Cambridge Companion to Levinas.* Cambridge: Cambridge University Press, xix.
7. Levinas (1987). Time and the Other and Additional Essays [*Le Temps et l'autre*]. Pittsburgh, Duquesne University Press.
8. Critchley and Bernasconi (2002). *The Cambridge Companion to Levinas.* Cambridge: Cambridge University Press, xxi.
9. Levinas (1978). Existence and Existents [*De l'existence à l'existant*]. The Hague, Nijhoff.
10. Levinas (2004). Totality and Infinity: An Essay on Exteriority [*Totalité et infini: essai sur l'extériorité*]. Pittsburgh, Duquesne University Press.
11. Levinas (1990). Difficult Freedom: Essays on Judaism [*Difficile liberté: essais sur le judaïsme*]. Baltimore, Johns Hopkins University Press.
12. Levinas (1998). Otherwise than Being: or Beyond Essence [*Autrement qu'être ou au-delà de l'essence*]. Pittsburgh, Duquesne University Press.

13. Critchley and Bernasconi (2002). *The Cambridge Companion to Levinas*. Cambridge: Cambridge University Press, xxvi. See Levinas (1990). *Nine Talmudic Readings* [From: *Quatre lectures talmudiques* and *Du sacré au saint*]. Bloomington: Indiana University Press.

Chapter 2

1. Generally, the French '*autrui*' is translated as 'Other' and '*autre*' is translated as 'other'. For Levinas, the highly personalized form of address in '*autrui*' focuses on a particular 'thou' or 'you', and therefore serves his turn to the otherness of the human subject more clearly than the more general term '*autre*'. For the purposes of the present discussion, the 'Other' will be used when referring explicitly to Levinas' own conceptualization of the term, and the 'other' will be used when referring more broadly to the other person without relying too strongly on Levinas' definition. It should be obvious, therefore, that it is appropriate to designate God as the 'Other'.

2. 'Secrecy and Freedom', in Levinas (1985). *Ethics and Infinity* [*Éthique et infini*]. Pittsburgh, Duquesne University Press, 80.

3. 'Preface', in Levinas (2004). *Totality and Infinity: An Essay on Exteriority* [*Totalité et infini: essai sur l'extériorité*]. Pittsburgh: Duquesne University Press, 21.

4. Ibid.

5. Again, the 'Other' is the personal other, the concrete *you*, whereas 'the other' is used as a more general identifying label. Often the two are strongly related and in any case, 'the Other' is central to all of Levinas' philosophy. Ibid., 24.

6. 'Preface', in Ibid., 28.

7. Ibid.

8. 'Preface', in Ibid., 29.

9. Ibid., 33.

10. Ibid.
11. Levinas cites Plato's concretization of need in examples such as the 'need to scratch oneself' in scabies or in sickness. See Plato (1993). *Philebus*. Indianapolis: Hackett, 46a. Levinas (2004). *Totality and Infinity: An Essay on Exteriority* [*Totalité et infini: essai sur l'extériorité*]. Pittsburgh: Duquesne University Press, 116.
12. Levinas (2004). *Totality and Infinity: An Essay on Exteriority* [*Totalité et infini: essai sur l'extériorité*]. Pittsburgh: Duquesne University Press, 116–7.
13. Ibid., 117.
14. Ibid.
15. Dedication, Levinas (1998). *Otherwise than Being: or Beyond Essence* [*Autrement qu'être ou au-delà de l'essence*]. Pittsburgh: Duquesne University Press.
16. Putnam, Hilary, 'Levinas and Judaism', in Critchley and Bernasconi (2002). *The Cambridge Companion to Levinas*. Cambridge: Cambridge University Press, 34.
17. Ward, Graham, 'On Time and Salvation', in Hand (1996). *Facing the Other: The Ethics of Emmanuel Levinas*. Richmond: Curzon, 157.
18. See Levinas (1987). *Time and the Other and Additional Essays* [*Le Temps et l'autre*]. Pittsburgh: Duquesne University Press.
19. Ward, Graham, 'On Time and Salvation', in Hand (1996). *Facing the Other: The Ethics of Emmanuel Levinas*. Richmond: Curzon, 168.
20. Levinas (1998). *Otherwise than Being: or Beyond Essence* [*Autrement qu'être ou au-delà de l'essence*]. Pittsburgh: Duquesne University Press, 1–5.
21. Graham Ward, 'On Time and Salvation: The Eschatology of Emmanuel Levinas', in Hand (1996). *Facing the Other: The Ethics of Emmanuel Levinas*. Richmond: Curzon, 157.
22. Husserl (1999). *Cartesian Meditations: An Introduction to Phenomenology*. Dordrecht: Kluwer Academic Publishers.

See also the important collaboration: Husserl and Fink (1995). *Sixth Cartesian Meditation: The Idea of a Transcendental Theory of Method.* Bloomington: Indiana University Press.

23. Levinas (1998). *Otherwise than Being: or Beyond Essence* [*Autrement qu'être ou au-delà de l'essence*]. Pittsburgh: Duquesne University Press, 47.

24. See 'The Other Side of Intentionality', in Nelson, Kapust and Still (2005). *Addressing Levinas.* Evanston: Northwestern University Press, 113.

25. Levinas (1998). *Otherwise than Being: or Beyond Essence* [*Autrement qu'être ou au-delà de l'essence*]. Pittsburgh: Duquesne University Press, 48.

26. For example, see Heidegger (1962). *Being and Time.* London: SCM, 264.

27. Schrijvers (2006). 'Ontotheological Turnings? Marion, Lacoste and Levinas on the Decentring of Modern Subjectivity'. *Modern Theology* 22(2): 245.

28. Levinas (1998). *Otherwise than Being: or Beyond Essence* [*Autrement qu'être ou au-delà de l'essence*]. Pittsburgh: Duquesne University Press, 181. Also at 109, 36 and 74.

29. Ibid., 90.

30. Ibid., 146.

31. Marion (2002). *Being Given: Toward a Phenomenology of Givenness.* Stanford: Stanford University Press, 266.

32. Ibid., 267.

33. Ibid.

34. See especially Ibid., 196–247. Also an extended treatment in Marion (2002). *In Excess: Studies of Saturated Phenomena.* New York: Fordham University Press.

35. Marion (2002). *Being Given: Toward a Phenomenology of Givenness.* Stanford: Stanford University Press, 228–33.

36. Ibid., 234.

37. Ibid., 231.

38. Ibid., 232.

39. Ibid.

40. Ibid., 235.

41. Ibid. This is a line that Marion elsewhere ignores. See for example: Marion (2002). 'They Recognized Him; And He Became Invisible To Them'. *Modern Theology* 18(2).

42. Marion (2002). *Being Given: Toward a Phenomenology of Givenness*. Stanford: Stanford University Press, 238.

43. Ibid.

44. Ibid., 241.

45. Marion (1991). *God without being: hors-texte*. Chicago: University of Chicago Press, 171.

46. See 'Humanism and An-archy', in Levinas (1987). *Collected Philosophical Papers*. Dordrecht: M. Nijhoff.

47. 'Humanism and An-archy', in Ibid., 132.

48. Marion (2002). *Being Given: Toward a Phenomenology of Givenness*. Stanford: Stanford University Press, 117.

49. John Henry Newman, *Praise to the Holiest in the Height*, sixth stanza, 1866.

50. Levinas (1998). *Otherwise than Being: or Beyond Essence* [*Autrement qu'être ou au-delà de l'essence*]. Pittsburgh: Duquesne University Press, 102–9.

Chapter 3

1. 'Philosophy, Justice, and Love', in Levinas (2001). *Is it Righteous to Be?: Interviews with Emmanuel Levinas*. Stanford: Stanford University Press, 171.

2. Levinas (2004). *Totality and Infinity: An Essay on Exteriority* [*Totalité et infini: essai sur l'extériorité*]. Pittsburgh: Duquesne University Press, 195.

3. See especially the English translation of Janicaud's original critique (*Le tournant théologique de la phenomenology française*) and various defences, which themselves were first published as *Phenomenology and Theology* (*Phénoménologie et théologie*) in 1992. Janicaud et al (2000). *Phenomenology and the 'theological turn': The French Debate*. New York: Fordham University Press. What makes the debate all the more interesting is that it was Levinas who first translated

Husserl's *Cartesian Meditations* in French in 1931, 7 years before the book was posthumously published in German under Husserl's name. It was Levinas who introduced German phenomenology into the French academy.

4. Husserl (1965). *Phenomenology and the Crisis of Philosophy.* New York: Harper, 72–4.
5. Ibid., 129.
6. Ibid., 147.
7. '*Zurück zu den Sachen selbst*'. See Husserl (1970). *Logical Investigations.* London: Routledge.
8. See Scheler (1973). *Formalism in Ethics and Non-formal Ethics of Values: A New Attempt Toward the Foundation of an Ethical Personalism.* Evanston: Northwestern University Press. Arendt (1999). *The Human Condition.* Chicago: University of Chicago Press.
9. Moran (2000). *Introduction to Phenomenology.* London: Routledge, xiv.
10. Spiegelberg and Schuhmann (1982). *The Phenomenological Movement: A Historical Introduction.* Hague: M. Nijhoff. Michael Purcell also draws on the same story with reference to Simone de Beauvoir's La Force de l'age, in Purcell (2006). *Levinas and Theology.* Cambridge: Cambridge University Press, 7–8.
11. See accounts in Beauvoir (1962). *The Prime of Life.* Cleveland: World. Also further elaboration in: Spiegelberg and Schuhmann (1982). *The Phenomenological Movement: A Historical Introduction.* Hague: M. Nijhoff.
12. Husserl's five Meditations were first given in two lectures in the Sorbonne at the Amphitheatre Descartes on 23 and 25 February 1929. See Husserl (1999). *Cartesian Meditations: An Introduction to Phenomenology.* Dordrecht: Kluwer Academic Publishers.
13. Ibid.
14. Levinas (2004). *Totality and Infinity: An Essay on Exteriority* [*Totalité et infini: essai sur l'extériorité*]. Pittsburgh: Duquesne University Press, 187.

15. Ibid., 198.
16. Ibid.
17. Ibid.
18. Ibid., 199.
19. Ibid.
20. Ibid., 281.
21. Ibid.
22. Marion (2007). *The Erotic Phenomenon.* Chicago: University of Chicago Press, 1.
23. Marion (2002). *In Excess: Studies of Saturated Phenomena.* New York: Fordham University Press.
24. Janicaud (2005). *Phenomenology 'wide open': After the French Debate.* New York: Fordham University Press, 64.
25. Primarily see: Marion (1991). *God without being: hors-texte.* Chicago: University of Chicago Press.
26. Horner (2001). *Rethinking God as Gift: Marion, Derrida, and the Limits of Phenomenology.* New York: Fordham University Press, 83.
27. Marion (2007). *The Erotic Phenomenon.* Chicago: University of Chicago Press, 167.
28. Marion (1998). *Reduction and Givenness: Investigations of Husserl, Heidegger, and Phenomenology.* Evanston: North western University Press. Marion (2002). *In Excess: Studies of Saturated Phenomena.* New York: Fordham University Press. Marion (2002). *Being Given: Toward a Phenomenology of Givenness.* Stanford: Stanford University Press.
29. Moran (2000). *Introduction to Phenomenology.* London: Routledge, xiii.
30. Levinas (1998). *Otherwise than Being: or Beyond Essence* [*Autrement qu'être ou au-delà de l'essence*]. Pittsburgh: Duquesne University Press, 155.
31. Purcell (2006). *Levinas and Theology.* Cambridge: Cambridge University Press, 60.
32. 'Who Shall Not Prophesy?', in Levinas (2001). *Is it Righteous to Be?: Interviews with Emmanuel Levinas.* Stanford: Stanford University Press, 223–4.

33. Levinas (2004). *Totality and Infinity: An Essay on Exteriority* [*Totalité et infini: essai sur l'extériorité*]. Pittsburgh: Duquesne University Press, 28.

34. 'Reality Has Weight', in Levinas (2001). *Is it Righteous to Be?: Interviews with Emmanuel Levinas*. Stanford: Stanford University Press, 159.

Chapter 4

1. Levinas, Emmanuel, 'Ethics as First Philosophy', in Levinas (1989). *The Levinas Reader*. Oxford: Blackwell, 75–87.

2. Levinas (1998). *Of God Who Comes to Mind* [*De Dieu qui vient à l'idée*]. Stanford: Stanford University Press, 61.

3. Ibid., 62.

4. Ibid., 62–4.

5. Ibid., 64.

6. Ibid., 69.

7. Ibid., 75.

8. 'In the Name of the Other', in Levinas (2001). *Is it Righteous to Be?: Interviews with Emmanuel Levinas*. Stanford: Stanford University Press, 192.

9. Horner, Robyn, 'Levinas's Gifts to Christian Theology', in Hart and Signer (2010). *The Exorbitant: Emmanuel Levinas between Jews and Christians*. New York: Fordham University Press, 140.

10. Horner, Robyn, 'Levinas's Gifts to Christian Theology', in Ibid., 141.

11. See especially: Purcell (1998). *Mystery and Method: The Other in Rahner and Levinas*. Milwaukee: Marquette.

12. Purcell (2003). '"Levinas and Theology"? The Scope and Limits of Doing Theology with Levinas'. *Heythrop Journal* XLIV(4): 476.

13. Roger Burggraeve, 'Responsibility Precedes Freedom: In Search of a Biblical-Philosophical Foundation of a Personalistic Love Ethic', in Janssens, Selling, Böckle and

Kelly (1988). *Personalist Morals: Essays in Honor of Professor Louis Janssens*. Leuven: Peeters, 121–8, 123, 131.

14. Burggraeve, Roger, "'No One Can Save Oneself without Others": *An Ethic of Liberation in the Footsteps of Emmanuel Levinas*', in Burggraeve (2008). *The Awakening to the Other: A Provocative Dialogue with Emmanuel Levinas*. Leuven: Peeters, 51.

15. Burggraeve, Roger, "'No One Can Save Oneself without Others": *An Ethic of Liberation in the Footsteps of Emmanuel Levinas*', Ibid., 63–4.

16. Horner, Robyn, 'Levinas's Gifts to Christian Theology', in Hart and Signer (2010). *The Exorbitant: Emmanuel Levinas between Jews and Christians*. New York: Fordham University Press, 146.

17. See especially Levinas (1998). *Otherwise than Being: or Beyond Essence [Autrement qu'être ou au-delà de l'essence]*. Pittsburgh: Duquesne University Press.

18. Marion (2002). *Being Given: Toward a Phenomenology of Givenness*. Stanford: Stanford University Press, 267.

19. See Marion, Jean-Luc, 'The Final Appeal of the Subject', in Caputo (2002). *The Religious*. Malden: Blackwell, 131–44. Marion (2007). *The Erotic Phenomenon*. Chicago: University of Chicago Press.

20. See especially Marion (2002). *In Excess: Studies of Saturated Phenomena*. New York: Fordham University Press. Marion (2002). *Being Given: Toward a Phenomenology of Givenness*. Stanford: Stanford University Press.

21. Horner, Robyn, 'Levinas's Gifts to Christian Theology', in Hart and Signer (2010). *The Exorbitant: Emmanuel Levinas between Jews and Christians*. New York: Fordham University Press, 146.

22. See especially Hart (2003). *The Beauty of the Infinite: The Aesthetics of Christian Truth*. Grand Rapids: Eerdmans, 43–93.

23. Ibid., 82.

24. Milbank (1999). 'The Ethics of Self Sacrifice'. *First Things* 91.

25. Ibid.

26. Levinas' account of death developed in close approximation to Jacques Derrida, who describes the impossibility of dying for another. The absolute sovereignty of the other person requires that each particular death is experienced in the singular, and any appeal to moral or figurative deaths for 'another' is impossible. According to Derrida: '*Tout Autre Est Tout Autre*' ['Every other is totally the other', or alternatively, 'every other (one) is every (bit) the other']. The gift of death is an impossible gift, even if, at times, it becomes a necessary action to perform. Derrida (2008). *The Gift of Death*. Chicago: University of Chicago Press.

27. See especially: Spaemann (2005). *Happiness and Benevolence*. T&T Clark.

28. Milbank (1999). 'The Ethics of Self Sacrifice'. *First Things* 91: 36.

29. Ibid., 38.

30. Eagleton (2009). *Trouble with Strangers: A Study of Ethics*. Chichester: Wiley-Blackwell, 231.

31. Augustine (1951). *Letters*. Washington: Catholic University of America Press. Letter, 130.

32. Balthasar (1989). *Explorations in Theology I: The Word Made Flesh*. San Francisco: Ignatius Press, 206.

33. Levinas, Emmanuel, 'Prayer Without Demand', in Levinas (1989). *The Levinas Reader*. Oxford: Blackwell, 227–34.

34. Ibid., 228.

35. Ibid., 228–9.

36. The book was also first published in Vilna, called 'Jerusalem of the East', a Lithuanian city not far from Levinas' birth town of Kaunas.

37. Levinas, Emmanuel, 'Prayer without Demand', in Levinas (1989). *The Levinas Reader*. Oxford: Blackwell, 229.

38. Ibid., 231.

39. Ibid.
40. Ibid.
41. Ibid.
42. Ibid.
43. Ibid.
44. Ibid.
45. Levinas, Emmanuel, 'Prayer without Demand', in Ibid., 232.
46. Levinas, Emmanuel, 'Freedom and Command', in Levinas (1987). *Collected Philosophical Papers*. Dordrecht: M. Nijhoff, 23.
47. See Sarah Allen's work for the contrast between the early Greek account of sense and being with that of Levinas. Allen (2009). *The Philosophical Sense of Transcendence: Levinas and Plato on Loving Beyond Being*. Pittsburgh: Duquesne University Press.
48. Levinas, Emmanuel, 'Prayer without Demand', in Levinas (1989). *The Levinas Reader*. Oxford: Blackwell, 233.
49. Ibid.
50. Ibid.
51. 'The Name of God According to a Few Talmudic Texts', in Levinas (1994). *Beyond the Verse: Talmudic Readings and Lectures* [*L'Au-delà du verset: Lectures et Discours Talmudique*]. Bloomington: Indiana University Press, 122.
52. Levinas, Emmanuel, 'Prayer without Demand', in Levinas (1989). *The Levinas Reader*. Oxford: Blackwell, 234.
53. Ibid.
54. Ibid.
55. Burggraeve, R., 'No one Can Save Oneself without Others: An Ethic of Liberation in the Footsteps of Emmanuel Levinas', in Burggraeve (2008). *The Awakening to the Other: A Provocative Dialogue with Emmanuel Levinas*. Leuven: Peeters, 13–65.
56. Burggraeve chiefly refers to Levinas' thought in the longer works: Levinas (1978). *Existence and Existents* [*De l'existence à l'existant*]. The Hague: Nijhoff. Levinas (1987). *Time and the*

Other and Additional Essays [*Le Temps et l'autre*]. Pittsburgh: Duquesne University Press. Levinas (1998). *Otherwise than Being: or Beyond Essence* [*Autrement qu'être ou au-delà de l'essence*]. Pittsburgh: Duquesne University Press. Levinas (2004). *Totality and Infinity: An Essay on Exteriority* [*Totalité et infini: essai sur l'extériorité*]. Pittsburgh: Duquesne University Press.

57. Burggraeve, R., 'No one Can Save Oneself without Others: An Ethic of Liberation in the Footsteps of Emmanuel Levinas', in Burggraeve (2008). *The Awakening to the Other: A Provocative Dialogue with Emmanuel Levinas*. Leuven: Peeters, 22–3.

58. Ibid., 14.

59. Some accounts signify this as John of the Cross.

60. Levinas (1998). *Entre nous: on thinking-of-the-other* [*Entre Nous: Essais sur le penser-à-lautre*]. New York: Columbia University Press, 76.

Chapter 5

1. Levinas, E, 'On the Jewish Reading of Scriptures', in Levinas (1994). *Beyond the Verse: Talmudic Readings and Lectures* [*L'Au-delà du verset: Lectures et Discours Talmudique*]. Bloomington: Indiana University Press, 115.

2. Ibid., 114.

3. Levinas (1993). *Outside the Subject* [*Hors sujet*]. London: Athlone.

4. See the essay, 'The Strings and the Wood: On the Jewish Reading of the Bible', in Ibid., 127.

5. 'The Strings and the Wood: On the Jewish Reading of the Bible', in Ibid., 129.

6. See especially Part II: Buber (2004). *I and thou*. London: Continuum.

7. Levinas, E., 'In Memory of Alphonse de Waelhens', in Levinas (1993). *Outside the Subject* [*Hors sujet*]. London: Athlone, 115.

8. Levinas, E., 'Apropos of Buber: Some Notes', in Ibid., 46.

Notes

9. Putnam (2008). *Jewish Philosophy as a Guide to Life: Rosenzweig, Buber, Lévinas, Wittgenstein.* Bloomington: Indiana University Press, 68.

10. Critchley, Simon, 'Leaving the Climate of Heidegger's Thinking', in Hansel (2009). *Levinas in Jerusalem: Phenomenology, Ethics, Politics, Aesthetics.* Dordrecht: Springer, 53.

11. 'Outside the Subject', in Levinas (1993). *Outside the Subject* [*Hors sujet*]. London: Athlone, 158.

12. Levinas, E., 'On the Jewish Reading of Scriptures', in Levinas (1994). *Beyond the Verse: Talmudic Readings and Lectures* [*L'Au-delà du verset: Lectures et Discours Talmudique*]. Bloomington: Indiana University Press, 101.

13. Levinas, E., 'On the Jewish Reading of Scriptures', in Ibid., 102.

14. 'On the Jewish Reading of Scriptures', in Ibid., 103.

15. Ibid.

16. 'On the Jewish Reading of Scriptures', in Ibid.

17. Ibid., 104.

18. Ibid., 105.

19. Ibid.

20. Ibid., 107.

21. Ibid.

22. Ibid.

23. Ibid., 110.

24. Ibid., 111.

25. Levinas, E., 'On the Jewish Reading of Scriptures', in Ibid.

26. Ibid.

27. Ibid., 115.

28. 'On the Jewish Reading of Scriptures', in Ibid.

29. Ibid.

30. Ibid., 114.

31. Ibid.

32. 'The State of Israel and the Religion of Israel', in Levinas (1990). *Difficult Freedom: Essays on Judaism* [*Difficile liberté: essais sur le judaïsme*]. Baltimore: Johns Hopkins University Press, 220.

33. 'The State of Israel and the Religion of Israel', in Ibid., 217.
34. Ibid., 218.
35. Ibid., 219.
36. 'Judaism and the Present', in Ibid., 212–3.
37. 'Ibid., 212–4.
38. 'Space is not One-Dimensional', in Ibid., 264.
39. Ibid., 263.
40. Ibid., 264.
41. Levinas, E., 'Politics After!', in Ibid., 190.
42. Levinas, E., 'The State of Caesar and the State of David', in Ibid., 186.
43. 'The State of Caesar and the State of David', in Ibid., 187.
44. 'Judaism and Christianity', in Levinas (1994). *In the Time of the Nations* [*A l'Heure des Nations*]. London: Athlone, 161–6.
45. 'Judaism and Christianity', in Ibid., 161.
46. Ibid., 162.
47. Ibid.
48. Ibid.
49. Ibid., 163.
50. Rosenzweig (2005). *The Star of Redemption*. Madison: University of Wisconsin Press.
51. Levinas, E., 'Judaism and Christianity', in Levinas (1994). *In the Time of the Nations* [*A l'Heure des Nations*]. London: Athlone, 163.
52. Ibid., 166.
53. 'Glory of the Infinite and Witnessing', in Levinas (2000). *God, Death and Time* [*Dieu, la mort et le temps*]. Stanford: Stanford University Press, 195.
54. Morgan (2007). *Discovering Levinas*. Cambridge: Cambridge University Press, 336.
55. Ibid., 340–7.
56. 'Humanism and An-Archy', in Levinas (1987). *Collected Philosophical Papers*. Dordrecht: M. Nijhoff, 131.
57. 'God and Philosophy', in Ibid., 154.
58. Ibid., 160.

59. See Descartes' third Meditation: Descartes (1996). *Meditations on First Philosophy: With Selections from the Objections and Replies*. New York: Cambridge University Press.

60. 'A Religion for Adults', in Levinas (1990). *Difficult Freedom: Essays on Judaism [Difficile liberté: essais sur le judaïsme]*. Baltimore: Johns Hopkins University Press, 11–13.

61. 'A Religion for Adults', in Ibid., 12.

62. Ibid., 14.

63. Peperzak (1997). *Beyond: The Philosophy of Emmanuel Levinas*. Evanston: Northwestern University Press, 26–7.

64. 'A Religion for Adults', in Levinas (1990). *Difficult Freedom: Essays on Judaism [Difficile liberté: essais sur le judaïsme]*. Baltimore: Johns Hopkins University Press, 21.

65. 'Between Two Worlds', in Ibid., 197.

66. Levinas says as much in 'Exclusive Rights', in Ibid., 240.

67. 'Israel and Universalism', in Ibid., 176.

68. Cohen, Richard A., 'Against Theology, or "The Devotion of a Theology Without Theodicy"', in Hart and Signer (2010). *The Exorbitant: Emmanuel Levinas between Jews and Christians*. New York: Fordham University Press, 87.

69. 'The Nations and the Presence of Israel', in Levinas (1994). *In the Time of the Nations [A l'Heure des Nations]*. London: Athlone, 108.

70. Ibid.

Chapter 6

1. Levinas (1998). *Otherwise than Being: or Beyond Essence [Autrement qu'être ou au-delà de l'essence]*. Pittsburgh: Duquesne University Press, Dedication.

2. Morgan (2011). *The Cambridge Introduction to Emmanuel Levinas*. Cambridge: Cambridge University Press, 32–3.

3. 'Transcendence and Evil', in Levinas (1987). *Collected Philosophical Papers*. Dordrecht: M. Nijhoff, 180.

4. Job has been described as a defining myth for Western civilization in Schreiner (1994). *Where Shall Wisdom be Found?: Calvin's Exegesis of Job from Medieval and Modern Perspectives.* Chicago: University of Chicago Press. See also Manley (1997). *Wisdom, Let Us Attend: Job, the Fathers, and the Old Testament.* Menlo Park: Monastery Books. Fisher (2009). *The Many Voices of Job.* Eugene: Cascade Books. Dell (2010). *Ethical and Unethical in the Old Testament: God and Humans in Dialogue.* New York: T&T Clark.

5. Levinas wrote a forward to this book. See Nemo and Lévinas (1998). *Job and the Excess of Evil.* Pittsburgh: Duquesne University Press.

6. 'Transcendence and Evil', in Levinas (1987). *Collected Philosophical Papers.* Dordrecht: M. Nijhoff, 179.

7. Ibid., 181.

8. Levinas (1990). *Nine Talmudic Readings* [From: *Quatre lectures talmudiques* and *Du sacré au saint*]. Bloomington: Indiana University Press, 85.

9. See *The Principles of Nature and Grace, Based on Reason*: Leibniz (1998). *Philosophical Texts.* Oxford: Oxford University Press.

10. 'Transcendence and Evil', in Levinas (1987). *Collected Philosophical Papers.* Dordrecht: M. Nijhoff, 182.

11. Ibid., 183.

12. Ibid., 184.

13. Chrétien (1991). *La dette et l'élection. Cahier de l'Herne, Emmanuel Lévinas.* Paris: Editions de l'Herne.

14. Ibid., 268.

15. 'Transcendence and Evil', in Levinas (1987). *Collected Philosophical Papers.* Dordrecht: M. Nijhoff, 185.

16. Ibid.

17. Ibid., 186.

18. Levinas (2004). *Totality and Infinity: An Essay on Exteriority* [*Totalité et infini: essai sur l'extériorité*]. Pittsburgh: Duquesne University Press, 78.

19. Ibid., 180.

20. Ibid., 78.
21. Ibid., 76.
22. Ibid., 78.
23. Ibid., 79.
24. See Levinas' rejection of mediation as the imperialistic closing of distance in Ibid., 44. Also his reconstruction of participation as the movement towards the alterity of the other through an ethical desire, in the same work (61).
25. Westphal, Merold, 'Thinking about God and God-Talk with Levinas', in Hart and Signer (2010). *The Exorbitant: Emmanuel Levinas between Jews and Christians.* New York: Fordham University Press, 223.
26. 'Signification and Sense', in Levinas (2006). *Humanism of the Other* [*Humanisme de l'autre homme*]. Urbana: University of Illinois Press, 44.
27. See especially the discussion in O'Donovan (2005). *The Ways of Judgment.* Grand Rapids: Eerdmans, 88–94. This is explained by O'Donovan as a crucial event in the life of a singular human being, which carries social and political consequences.
28. Milbank (2003). *Being Reconciled: Ontology and Pardon.* London: Routledge, 138.
29. Ibid., 100.
30. See the dismantling of traditional notions of Being, and the inclusion of 'participation' in that reconstruction, in Levinas (2004). *Totality and Infinity: An Essay on Exteriority* [*Totalité et infini: essai sur l'extériorité*]. Pittsburgh: Duquesne University Press, 60–1.
31. Levinas (1998). *Entre nous: on thinking-of-the-other* [*Entre Nous: Essais sur le penser-à-lautre*]. New York: Columbia University Press, 245.
32. Levinas (2004). *Totality and Infinity: An Essay on Exteriority* [*Totalité et infini: essai sur l'extériorité*]. Pittsburgh: Duquesne University Press, 78.
33. Ibid.

Notes

34. Lubac (1982). *The Motherhood of the Church*. San Francisco: Ignatius Press, 113.
35. Scholars agree his birth sits somewhere between 296 and 298.
36. Athanasius (1993). *On the Incarnation: The Treatise De Incarnatione Verbi Dei*. Crestwood: St Vladimir's Seminary Press.
37. Ibid., 54–3.
38. Ibid., 12–13.
39. Weinandy (2007). *Athanasius: A Theological Introduction*. Aldershot: Ashgate, 31–4.
40. Pettersen (1995). *Athanasius*. Harrisburg: Morehouse, 136–90, Weinandy (2007). *Athanasius: A Theological Introduction*. Aldershot: Ashgate, 103–19.
41. Weinandy (2007). *Athanasius: A Theological Introduction*. Aldershot: Ashgate, 100.
42. Augustine (2000). Expositions of the Psalms (33–50), The Works of Saint Augustine. Vol III/16. Translator: Maria Boulding OSB. New York: New City, p. 381.
43. Thomas Aquinas (1964). *Summa theologiae*. London: Blackfriars & Eyre & Spottiswoode, III, q. 1 a. 2.
44. See Velde (1995). *Participation and Substantiality in Thomas Aquinas*. Leiden: E. J. Brill, Zizioulas (2006). *Communion and Otherness*. New York: Continuum.
45. Levinas (1998). *Otherwise than Being: or Beyond Essence* [*Autrement qu'être ou au-delà de l'essence*]. Pittsburgh: Duquesne University Press, 147.
46. Ibid., 144.
47. Ibid., 144–5.
48. Blum (2000). 'Overcoming Relativism? Levinas's Return to Platonism.' *Journal of Religious Ethics* 28(1): 101.
49. Morgan (2007). *Discovering Levinas*. Cambridge: Cambridge University Press, 190.
50. Levinas (1998). *Otherwise than Being: or Beyond Essence* [*Autrement qu'être ou au-delà de l'essence*]. Pittsburgh: Duquesne University Press, 136–40.

51. See 'Sensibility, Trauma, and the Trace: Levinas from Phenomenology to the Immemorial' by Michael Newman in, Bloechl (2000). *The Face of the Other and the Trace of God: Essays on the Philosophy of Emmanuel Levinas.* New York: Fordham University Press, 91.
52. Merold Westphal, 'Thinking about God and God-Talk with Levinas', in Hart and Signer (2010). *The Exorbitant: Emmanuel Levinas between Jews and Christians.* New York: Fordham University Press, 225.
53. Wyschogrod (2000). *Emmanuel Levinas: The Problem of Ethical Metaphysics.* New York: Fordham University Press, 87.
54. Ibid., 105.
55. Ibid., 108.
56. Bloechl, Jeffrey, 'Ethics as First Philosophy and Religion', in Bloechl (2000). *The Face of the Other and the Trace of God: Essays on the Philosophy of Emmanuel Levinas.* New York: Fordham University Press, 145.
57. Levinas (1998). *Of God Who Comes to Mind* [*De Dieu qui vient à l'idée*]. Stanford: Stanford University Press.
58. 'God and Philosophy', in Ibid., 55–78.
59. Ibid., 56.
60. Ibid., 57.
61. Ibid., 58.
62. Ibid., 59.
63. Ibid., 72.
64. Ibid., 77.
65. 'Hermeneutics and Beyond', in Ibid., 100–10.
66. See Michael Weston's essay, 'Kierkegaard, Levinas, and "Absolute Alterity"', in Simmons and Wood (2008). *Kierkegaard and Levinas: Ethics, Politics, and Religion.* Bloomington: Indiana University Press, 153–68. The relevance of Kierkegaard to contemporary debate is increasingly acknowledged. Of particular interest is his account of the experiential nature of the human condition as it perceives and responds to alterity, for

example: Kierkegaard (1992). *Either/or: A Fragment of Life.* London: Penguin. Kierkegaard (2006). *Fear and Trembling.* Cambridge: Cambridge University Press.

67. 'Hermeneutics and Beyond', in Levinas (1998). *Of God Who Comes to Mind* [*De Dieu qui vient à l'idée*]. Stanford: Stanford University Press, 108.

68. See for example Book XII, Chapter 8: Augustine (1998). *De Civitate Dei: The City of God Against the Pagans.* Cambridge: Cambridge University Press.

69. See Lk 23: 34, Lk 23: 43, Lk 19: 26-27, Matt 27: 46, Mk 15: 34, Jn 19: 28, Jn 19: 30, Lk 23: 46.

70. 'Transcendence and Evil', in Levinas (1998). *Of God Who Comes to Mind* [*De Dieu qui vient à l'idée*]. Stanford: Stanford University Press, 132.

71. 'Witnessing and Ethics', in Levinas (2000). *God, Death and Time* [*Dieu, la mort et le temps*]. Stanford: Stanford University Press, 200.

Chapter 7

1. Levinas (1998). *Of God Who Comes to Mind* [*De Dieu qui vient à l'idée*]. Stanford: Stanford University Press, 69.

2. See especially Anselm's *Proslogium*, in which he outlines a rational description of God in what became a controversial position in succeeding theological debate. Anselm (1962). *Basic Writings: Proslogium; Monologium; Gaunilon's on Behalf of the Fool; Cur deus homo.* La Salle: Open Court.

3. Levinas (1989). *The Levinas Reader.* Oxford: Blackwell, 233.

4. John Paul II (1994). *Crossing the Threshold of Hope.* London: Cape, 36.

5. 'On the Jewish Reading of Scriptures', in Levinas (1994). *Beyond the Verse: Talmudic Readings and Lectures* [*L'Au-delà du verset: Lectures et Discours Talmudique*]. Bloomington: Indiana University Press, 115.

Bibliography

Allen, S. (2009). *The Philosophical Sense of Transcendence: Levinas and Plato on Loving Beyond Being*. Pittsburgh: Duquesne University Press.

Anselm (1962). *Basic Writings: Proslogium; Monologium; Gaunilon's on Behalf of the Fool; Cur deus homo*. La Salle: Open Court.

Arendt, H. (1999). *The Human Condition*. Chicago: University of Chicago Press.

Athanasius (1993). *On the Incarnation: The Treatise De Incarnatione Verbi Dei*. Crestwood: St Vladimir's Seminary Press.

Augustine (1951). *Letters*. Washington: Catholic University of America Press.

— (1998). *De Civitate Dei: The City of God Against the Pagans*. Cambridge: Cambridge University Press.

— (2007). *Essential Sermons*. Hyde Park: New City Press.

Balthasar, H. U. v. (1989). *Explorations in Theology I: The Word Made Flesh*. San Francisco: Ignatius Press.

Beauvoir, S. d. (1962). *The Prime of Life*. Cleveland: World.

Bloechl, J. (2000). *The Face of the Other and the Trace of God: Essays on the Philosophy of Emmanuel Levinas*. New York: Fordham University Press.

Blum, P. C. (2000). 'Overcoming Relativism? Levinas's Return to Platonism'. *Journal of Religious Ethics* 28(1): 91–117.

Brague, R. (1995). 'The Impotence of the Word: The God Who has Said It All'. *Diogenes* 43/2(170): 43–67.

Buber, M. (2004). *I and thou*. London: Continuum.

Burggraeve, R. (2008). *The Awakening to the Other: A Provocative Dialogue with Emmanuel Levinas*. Leuven: Peeters.

Bibliography

Caputo, J. D. (2002). *The Religious*. Malden: Blackwell.

Chrétien, J.-L. (1991). *La dette et l'élection. Cahier de l'Herne, Emmanuel Lévinas*. Paris: Editions de l'Herne.

Critchley, S. and R. Bernasconi (2002). *The Cambridge Companion to Levinas*. Cambridge: Cambridge University Press.

Dell, K. J. (2010). *Ethical and Unethical in the Old Testament: God and Humans in Dialogue*. New York: T&T Clark.

Derrida, J. (2008). *The Gift of Death*. Chicago: University of Chicago Press.

Descartes, R. (1996). *Meditations on First Philosophy: With Selections from the Objections and Replies*. New York: Cambridge University Press.

Eagleton, T. (2009). *Trouble with Strangers: A Study of Ethics*. Chichester: Wiley-Blackwell.

Fisher, L. R. (2009). *The Many Voices of Job*. Eugene: Cascade Books.

Hand, S. (1996). *Facing the Other: The Ethics of Emmanuel Levinas*. Richmond: Curzon.

Hansel, J. (2009). *Levinas in Jerusalem: Phenomenology, Ethics, Politics, Aesthetics*. Dordrecht: Springer.

Hart, D. B. (2003). *The Beauty of the Infinite: The Aesthetics of Christian Truth*. Grand Rapids: Eerdmans.

Hart, K. and M. A. Signer (2010). *The Exorbitant: Emmanuel Levinas between Jews and Christians*. New York: Fordham University Press.

Heidegger, M. (1962). *Being and Time*. London: SCM.

Horner, R. (2001). *Rethinking God as Gift: Marion, Derrida, and the Limits of Phenomenology*. New York: Fordham University Press.

Husserl, E. (1965). *Phenomenology and the Crisis of Philosophy*. New York: Harper.

Bibliography

— (1970). *Logical Investigations*. London: Routledge.

— (1999). *Cartesian Meditations: An Introduction to Phenomenology*. Dordrecht: Kluwer Academic Publishers.

Husserl, E. and E. Fink (1995). *Sixth Cartesian Meditation: The Idea of a Transcendental Theory of Method*. Bloomington: Indiana University Press.

Janicaud, D. (2005). *Phenomenology 'wide open': After the French Debate*. New York: Fordham University Press.

Janicaud, D., et al. (2000). *Phenomenology and the 'theological turn': The French Debate*. New York: Fordham University Press.

Janssens, L., J. A. Selling, et al. (1988). *Personalist Morals: Essays in Honor of Professor Louis Janssens*. Leuven: Peeters.

John Paul II (1994). *Crossing the Threshold of Hope*. London: Cape.

Kierkegaard, S. (1992). *Either/or: A Fragment of Life*. London: Penguin.

— (2006). *Fear and Trembling*. Cambridge: Cambridge University Press.

Leibniz, G. W. (1998). *Philosophical Texts*. Oxford: Oxford University Press.

Levinas, E. (1978). *Existence and Existents [De l'existence à l'existant]*. The Hague: Nijhoff.

— (1985). *Ethics and Infinity [Éthique et infini]*. Pittsburgh: Duquesne University Press.

— (1987). *Collected Philosophical Papers*. Dordrecht: M. Nijhoff.

— (1987). *Time and the Other and Additional Essays [Le Temps et l'autre]*. Pittsburgh: Duquesne University Press.

— (1989). *The Levinas Reader*. Oxford: Blackwell.

— (1990). *Difficult Freedom: Essays on Judaism [Difficile liberté: essais sur le judaïsme]*. Baltimore: Johns Hopkins University Press.

— (1990). *Nine Talmudic Readings [From: Quatre lectures talmudiques and Du sacré au saint]*. Bloomington: Indiana University Press.

— (1993). *Outside the Subject [Hors sujet]*. London: Athlone.

— (1994). *Beyond the Verse:Talmudic Readings and Lectures [L'Audelà du verset: Lectures et Discours Talmudique]*. Bloomington: Indiana University Press.

— (1994). *In the Time of the Nations [A l'Heure des Nations]*. London: Athlone.

— (1998). *Entre nous: on thinking-of-the-other [Entre Nous: Essais sur le penser-à-lautre]*. New York: Columbia University Press.

— (1998). *Of God Who Comes to Mind [De Dieu qui vient à l'idée]*. Stanford: Stanford University Press.

— (1998). *Otherwise than Being: or Beyond Essence [Autrement qu'être ou au-delà de l'essence]*. Pittsburgh: Duquesne University Press.

— (2000). *God, Death and Time [Dieu, la mort et le temps]*. Stanford: Stanford University Press.

— (2001). *Is it Righteous to Be?: Interviews with Emmanuel Levinas*. Stanford: Stanford University Press.

— (2003). *De l'évasion: On Escape*. Stanford: Stanford University Press.

— (2004). *Totality and Infinity:An Essay on Exteriority [Totalité et infini: essai sur l'extériorité]*. Pittsburgh: Duquesne University Press.

— (2006). *Humanism of the Other [Humanisme de l'autre homme]*. Urbana: University of Illinois Press.

— (2009). *Œuvres: Tome 1, Carnets de captivité: suivi de Écrits sur la captivité; et, Notes philosophiques diverses*. Paris: Grasset & Fasquelle.

Lubac, H. d. (1982). *The Motherhood of the Church*. San Francisco: Ignatius Press.

Malka, S. (2006). *Emmanuel Levinas: His Life and Legacy*. Pittsburgh: Duquesne University Press.

Bibliography

Manley, J. (1997). *Wisdom, Let Us Attend: Job, the Fathers, and the Old Testament*. Menlo Park: Monastery Books.

Marion, J.-L. (1991). *God without being: hors-texte*, Chicago: University of Chicago Press.

— (1998). *Reduction and Givenness: Investigations of Husserl, Heidegger, and Phenomenology*. Evanston: Northwestern University Press.

— (2002). *Being Given: Toward a Phenomenology of Givenness*. Stanford: Stanford University Press.

— (2002). *In Excess: Studies of Saturated Phenomena*. New York: Fordham University Press.

— (2002). 'They Recognized Him; And He Became Invisible To Them'. *Modern Theology* 18(2): 145–52.

— (2007). *The Erotic Phenomenon*. Chicago: University of Chicago Press.

Milbank, J. (1999). 'The Ethics of Self Sacrifice'. *First Things* 91: 33–8.

— (2003). *Being Reconciled: Ontology and Pardon*. London: Routledge.

Moran, D. (2000). *Introduction to Phenomenology*. London: Routledge.

Morgan, M. L. (2007). *Discovering Levinas*. Cambridge: Cambridge University Press.

— (2011). *The Cambridge Introduction to Emmanuel Levinas*. Cambridge: Cambridge University Press.

Nelson, E. S., A. Kapust, et al. (2005). *Addressing Levinas*. Evanston Northwestern University Press.

Nemo, P. and E. Lévinas (1998). *Job and the Excess of Evil*. Pittsburgh: Duquesne University Press.

O'Donovan, O. (2005). *The Ways of Judgment*. Grand Rapids: Eerdmans.

Peperzak, A. T. (1997). *Beyond: The Philosophy of Emmanuel Levinas*. Evanston: Northwestern University Press.

Pettersen, A. (1995). *Athanasius*. Harrisburg: Morehouse.

Plato (1993). *Philebus.* Indianapolis: Hackett.

Purcell, M. (1998). *Mystery and Method: The Other in Rahner and Levinas.* Milwaukee: Marquette.

— (2003). "'Levinas and Theology?" The Scope and Limits of Doing Theology with Levinas'. *Heythrop Journal* XLIV(4): 468–79.

— (2006). *Levinas and Theology.* Cambridge: Cambridge University Press.

Putnam, H. (2008). *Jewish Philosophy as a Guide to Life: Rosenzweig, Buber, Lévinas, Wittgenstein.* Bloomington: Indiana University Press.

Rosenzweig, F. (2005). *The Star of Redemption.* Madison: University of Wisconsin Press.

Scheler, M. (1973). *Formalism in Ethics and Non-formal Ethics of Values: A New Attempt Toward the Foundation of an Ethical Personalism.* Evanston: Northwestern University Press.

Schreiner, S. E. (1994). *Where Shall Wisdom be Found?: Calvin's Exegesis of Job from Medieval and Modern Perspectives.* Chicago: University of Chicago Press.

Schrijvers, J. (2006). 'Ontotheological Turnings? Marion, Lacoste and Levinas on the Decentring of Modern Subjectivity'. *Modern Theology* 22(2): 222–53.

Simmons, J. A. and D. Wood (2008). *Kierkegaard and Levinas: Ethics, Politics, and Religion.* Bloomington: Indiana University Press.

Spaemann, R. (2005). *Happiness and Benevolence.* Edinburgh: T&T Clark.

Spiegelberg, H. and K. Schuhmann (1982). *The Phenomenological Movement: A Historical Introduction.* Hague: M. Nijhoff.

Thomas Aquinas (1964). *Summa theologiae.* London: Blackfriars & Eyre & Spottiswoode.

Velde, R. A. t. (1995). *Participation and Substantiality in Thomas Aquinas.* Leiden: E. J. Brill.

Weinandy, T. G. (2007). *Athanasius: A Theological Introduction.* Aldershot: Ashgate.

Wyschogrod, E. (2000). *Emmanuel Levinas: The Problem of Ethical Metaphysics.* New York: Fordham University Press.

Zizioulas, J. D. (2006). *Communion and Otherness.* New York: Continuum.

Index

Abraham vii, 40, 117, 122, 142
alterity vii, 4–6, 13–16, 18–19,
     21–5, 27, 33–4, 37–8, 41–2,
     44–5, 50–2, 54, 56–7, 59, 62,
     65–7, 69–70, 73, 76–8, 80,
     82, 92, 95–6, 99–100, 106,
     108–10, 118–19, 121–2,
     125–6, 137–8, 141, 144–5,
     147–50, 153–4, 157–8, 160
Anselm, St 161
Arendt, Hannah 10, 46
Aristotle 5
Aron, Raymond 47
Athanasius, St 26, 139–40
Augustine, St 64, 82, 140–1, 150

Baird, Marie 72
Balthasar, Hans Urs von
     64, 72, 82
Barnes, Michael 72
Barth, Karl 64, 72
Beauchesne, Richard J. 72
Beauvoir, Simone de 47
Being 5, 12–13, 15, 19–21, 23,
     26, 33–7, 39, 54–5, 64–5,
     69–71, 75–6, 79, 85–6,
     88–9, 122, 125, 127, 131,
     142, 145–8, 151, 154, 158,
     160, 163
Bernier, J. F. 72
Bizeul, Yves 72
Blanchot, Maurice 2, 8, 14
Bloechl, Jeffrey 145
Brague, Rémi 4

Buber, Martin 99–101, 162
Burggraeve, Roger 72, 74–5,
     92–3

Cairns, Dorion 46
Calvin, John 64
Chouchani, Monsieur 9
Chrétien, Jean-Louis 42, 72, 131
Christ (also Jesus Christ, Jesus
     the Christ, Jesus of
     Nazareth) vii, 32–4,
     38–40, 58, 63, 79, 81, 91,
     118, 121, 136–41, 151–3,
     157, 159
Christianity ix, 62, 118–21,
     146, 154, 164
Cohen, Richard A. 125
communists 6
Congrad-Martius, Hedwig 46
Curkpatrick, Stephen 72

Dasein (also da-sein) 12–13
David Bentley-Hart 77, 80, 95
Deconstructionism (also
     deconstructionist) 1–2
de Lubac, Henri 138
Derrida, Jacque 1, 14, 78, 146
Descartes, René 13, 48, 59, 70,
     122–3
Desouche, Marie Thérèse 72
divinity vii, ix, 1, 39, 72, 88,
     90, 124, 132–5, 138–41,
     144–5, 148–9, 154, 157
Dostoevsky, Fyodor 148

Index

Dussell, Enrique 72
Eagleton, Terry 80
English (as a language) viii, 6, 11
epoché 21–2, 43, 48, 60
essence 13, 20, 43, 74, 87–8, 92,
  105, 124, 147, 150
Europe (also European) 4, 7,
  48, 59, 83, 112, 119, 121–2,
  127, 153, 163
Existentialism (also
  existentialist) 1, 2, 60

Farber, Marvin 46
Fink, Eugen 46
Ford, David F. 72
French
  as nationality or cultural vi,
    6–8, 10, 15, 42, 44, 47, 115
  as language 6, 9, 11, 47–8

German (as language) 6, 47
German National Socialism (also
  National Socialists) 2, 19,
  60, 127
God vii–ix, 2, 6, 11, 33–5, 37,
  39–42, 44–5, 54, 58–9, 61,
  64–6, 69–73, 75, 77–92,
  94, 96, 98, 100–13, 118–19,
  121–64
Goud, J. F. 72
Gurwitsch, Aron 46

Hart, Kevin 2
Henry, Michel 42
Heidegger (also
  Heideggerian) 5, 7–8,
  11–14, 25, 46–7, 49, 59
Holocaust viii, 2–3, 20, 119–20,
  122–3, 127–8, 132,
  149–50, 153–4, 163–4 *See
  also* Shoah

Horner, Robyn 54, 71–6
Husserl, Edmund (also Husserlian,
  Husserlians) 2, 5, 7, 9,
  13–14, 21–2, 27, 33, 44–8,
  59–61, 66, 149, 159

Incarnation of Jesus Christ
  39–40, 63, 65, 77, 94,
  135–6, 139–40, 159, 164
  incarnation 63, 135, 139, 164
Ingarden, Roman 46
inter-subjective (also
  inter-subjectivity) vii, 4,
  14, 24, 27, 42, 47, 52–3, 74,
  80, 145, 150, 157, 164
Irenaeus, St 64
Isaac vii, 40, 122, 142
Israel
  Modern State 9, 112–13,
    115–18, 154
  nation 83, 90, 97, 101–3,
    105, 107–8, 110, 112,
    114–17, 123–6, 139, 162–3
  people of (biblical) vii, 86, 90

Jacob vii, 40, 122, 142
Janicaud, Dominique 2, 42, 44,
  53, 61
Jaspers, Karl 46
Jew (also, Jews) 2, 8, 20, 99, 113,
  115–16, 122–5, 127, 139, 161
Jewish (also Judaic) viii, 2–3,
  6–11, 20, 60, 82–3, 87, 97,
  99–101, 103–6, 108–9,
  112–17, 119–27, 139, 142,
  145, 153, 162–3
Judaism ix, 6, 83, 86, 89, 97,
  99, 101, 113–15, 117–18,
  120–1, 125–6, 164
John Paul II (also Karol
  Wojtyla) 2, 14, 162
Jüngel, Eberhard 72

Index

Kabbalah 83–4, 86
Kierkegaard, Søren 149
Kyongsuk Min, Anselm 72

Lacoste, Jean-Yves 14
Landgrebe, Ludwig 46
Lavigne, J. F. 72
Leibniz, Gottfried 130
Lithuania (also Lithuanian) 6–8, 83, 118
Livingston, David J. 72
Lonergan, Bernard 72
Luther, Martin 64

Malka, Saloman 6
Marion, Jean-Luc 2, 14, 26–38, 42, 44–5, 52–5, 72, 75–8, 158–9
Marxism 60
Merleau-Ponty, Maurice 48
metaphysics (also metaphysical) 16–20, 35–7, 44, 53–4, 72, 83, 120–1, 130, 135, 141, 144, 162
Milbank, John 78–80, 95, 136
Moran, Dermot 46
Morgan, Michael 121–3, 128
Morrison, Glenn 72
Moses vii, 143

Nazi (Nazi pogroms) 3–4, 6, 8
Nihilist 2
Nemo, Philippe 129
Nerson, Henri 9
Newman, John Henry 39
Newman, Michael 142

ontology (also ontological) 13–15, 19–20, 23, 42, 49, 54, 69, 78–80, 85, 106, 122, 126, 130, 135, 146–8, 158

onto-theology 75, 80, 148, 160
Other (the Other) 1, 5–6, 12–16, 20–7, 30–1, 35–41, 44, 46–7, 49–52, 54–7, 61, 64, 66, 69–71, 73–8, 80–2, 87, 91, 93–7, 100–1, 108–10, 118, 121, 124–8, 130–5, 137–8, 140–4, 147–9, 151, 153–4, 158–61

Patocka, Jan 78
Peperzak, Adriaan 124
Pfeiffer, Gabrielle 9
phenomenological 2, 4, 6–7, 10, 16, 21–2, 24, 26–7, 30–1, 34–5, 40, 43–9, 52–4, 56–8, 60–2, 65, 76–7, 101, 107, 146, 151, 158, 160
phenomenologist(s) 2, 28, 44, 47, 60–1
phenomenology ix, 7, 14, 16, 28, 31, 33–4, 42–8, 52–5, 59–62, 66, 75, 146, 149, 157, 159
Plato 5, 36, 110–11, 142, 160
Plotinus 142
Poche, F. 72
Purcell, Michael 64, 72–3

Rahner, Karl 64, 72–3
Ricœur, Paul 2, 14, 162
Rosenzweig, Franz 16, 99, 120–1

Saracino, Michele 72–3
Sartre, Jean-Paul 1, 7, 47–8, 60
Scannone, Juan Carlos 72
Scheler, Max 46
Schrijvers, Joeri 24–5
Schütz, Alfred 46
Schuurman, Lamberto 72

Index

Scripture   vii, ix, 10, 34–5,
    64, 66, 81, 86–7, 90, 95,
    97–101, 103, 105–17,
    121–2, 124–5, 145, 154,
    160, 162–3, 165
Shoah   2, 20, 120, 150
Simonn, Derek   72
Smith, Steven G.   72
Sorbonne   9, 11
Spaemann, Robert   79
Stein, Edith   46, 60
Strandjord, J. P.   72

Tallon, Andrew   72
Talmud (also Talmudic)   2, 9–11,
    14, 74, 83, 86, 90, 97, 99,
    101–3, 118, 125
Talmudic   9–11, 14, 83, 86, 97,
    99, 101, 103, 118, 125
Thomas Aquinas, St   64, 93,
    140–1
Torah   2, 83, 86, 89, 97, 117
trace   1, 35, 37, 50–2, 135,
    141–3, 161

transcendent (also transcendence,
    transcends)   15, 17, 19,
    22, 24–5, 37, 39, 41, 45,
    47–8, 50–4, 56, 58–9, 61,
    63–4, 70, 73–4, 98, 101–2,
    105, 107–11, 117, 125,
    128, 132–3, 137–8, 146–9,
    151, 160

Vahanian, Gabriel   72
Vanderveldem, Guy   72
Vannin, M.   72
Veling, Terry A.   72
Volozhiner, Hayyim   82–8, 91

Ward, Graham   72
Webb, Stephen   72
Westphal, Merold   143
Wiesel, Elie   9
Wohlmuth, Josefin   72
World War II   2, 112, 127, 163
Wyschogrod, Edith   143–5

Ziarek, Krzystof   72

Biblical References

Acts	3:13	vii		1:17	vii
	17:22-34	62		18:6-7	32
	22:15	63		21:25	33
	22:16	63			
	22:18	63	Lev	18	105
Col	1:24	153	Lk	11:2-4	81
Deut	6:4	139	Matt	4:18-20	58
	6:5	87		6:9-13	81
	10:18	133		25	118
	25:2-3	102		27:46	152
	25:3	103			
			Mk	10: 17-22	33
Ex	3:1-21	143		15:34	152
	34:7	104			
			Prov	15:8	88
Gen	1:27	85			
	2:7	82, 85	Ps	22	152
				91:15	90
Is	45:7	151		141:2	81
	51:16	85			
	58	118	Psalm	82:5	86
	63:9	90			
			2 Peter	1:4	138
Job	1	129			
	2:9	150	Rom	8:26	81
	14:17	150			
	36:26	129	1 Sam	120	
	38:4	130, 131			
			1 Thes	5:17	81
Jn	1:5	93			
	10:10	136	Zechariah	7:8-10	133